CONTENTS

IMPORTANT NOTE TO READERS

This book has been written as a guide to the types of employment available within the child-care sector. The search for employment, job applications and guidance on terms and conditions are all included. Users of this book should note that any advice offered within the text is for guidance only, and the publishers and authors accept no responsibility for any loss occasioned to any person using or relying on any of the material within.

ABOUT THE AUTHORS

Christine Hobart and Jill Frankel come from a background of health visiting and nursery education. They worked together in Camden before meeting again at City and Islington College. They have worked together for many years, training students to work with young children and have written 12 books encompassing all areas of the child-care curriculum. Christine is an external examiner for CACHE.

Miranda Walker has worked with children from birth to 16 years in a range of settings, including her own day nursery and out-of-school clubs. She has inspected nursery provision for Ofsted, and worked at East Devon College as an Early Years and Playwork lecturer and NVQ assessor and internal verifier. She is a regular contributor to industry magazines and an established author.

Christine Hobart
Jill Frankel

Series Editor: Miranda Walker

nes

Text © Christine Hobart, Jill Frankel and Miranda Walker 2009

Original line drawings © Stanley Thornes (Publishers) Ltd 1996

The right of Christine Hobart, Jill Frankel and Miranda Walker to be identified as authors of this work has been asserted by them in accordance with the Copyright, Designs and Patents Act 1988.

The copyright holders authorise only users of *A Practical Guide to Child Care Employment* to make photocopies of pages 16, 20, 24, 25, 67, 68, 69 and 113 for their own immediate use within the child-care context.

No other rights are granted without permission in writing from the publishers or under licence from the Copyright Licensing Agency Limited. Further details of such licences (for reprographic reproduction) may be obtained from the Copyright Licensing Agency Limited, of Saffron House, 6–10 Kirby Street, London EC1N 8TS.

Copy by any other means or for any other purpose is strictly prohibited without the prior written consent of the copyright holders.

Applications for such permission should be addressed to the publishers.

First published in 1996 by:
Stanley Thornes (Publishers) Ltd

This edition published 2009 by:
Nelson Thornes Ltd
27 Bath Road
Cheltenham
GL53 7TH
United Kingdom

09 10 11 12 13 / 10 9 8 7 6 5 4 3 2 1

A catalogue record for this book is available from the British Library.

ISBN 978 1 4085 0485 7

Photographs on pages 79 and 88 © Fotolia
Front cover photograph © Bananastock/Punchstock
Typeset by Columns Design Ltd, Reading
Printed and bound in Spain by GraphyCems

INTRODUCTION

This book provides a comprehensive text for prospective child-care practitioners, describing the main types of jobs available, helping with job applications and interviews and showing how to settle into work patterns. We have pointed out the potential problems and highlighted good practice in a range of work settings, both in the public and the private sectors. Part of the book is devoted to helping employees understand their rights and employment procedures, shows how to deal with insurance and money matters, and discusses the benefits of joining a union.

Although written for all who wish to enter the area of child care from training, we have tried to make the book useful for people who are already working with children, who might wish to change jobs, who may be looking for further training or who may wish a change of direction.

Since the implementation of The Children Act, 1989, people wishing to employ child-care practitioners in the public sector are required to look for prospective employees with recognized qualifications in addition to suitable personal qualities and experience. There are some possibilities of employment in the private sector for people without qualifications although, increasingly, parents look for nannies who have received training.

This book is suitable for anyone looking for employment in a child-care setting. Most people reading this book will be about to gain an NVQ at Level 2 or Level 3, or to complete an equivalent child-care course, such as the CACHE Certificate/Diploma in Child Care and Education, or the BTEC National Certificate/Diploma in Children's Care, Learning and Development.

ACKNOWLEDGEMENTS

We would like to thank our colleagues in the Childcare Curriculum Area at City and Islington College for their support and encouragement.

A special thank you goes to Susan Hay Nursery Works Limited for allowing us to use the grievance and disciplinary procedures; to London Borough of Ealing Council for allowing us to use their application form and job specification details; and to CACHE for their list of principles of professional practice for the child-care worker.

We would also like to thank the students we have taught over the years and the training supervisors who have ensured their success.

1 *EMPLOYMENT OPPORTUNITIES*

> **This chapter covers:**
> - Working individually
> - Working in a team
> - Working part-time
> - Other areas of employment
> - Assessing your own needs
> - Further reading

Working with young children offers a huge range of employment opportunities. In this chapter, we have attempted to outline the main areas of employment open to child-care practitioners at the start of their career. Any of the jobs described will enable you to gain good basic practice and consolidate your knowledge and skills. You may choose to work alone with children in a home setting or you may prefer to work as part of a team within an organization or establishment. We have pin-pointed the main advantages and disadvantages in each area of work.

Working individually

As a residential or daily nanny, as a mother's help or 'au pair', or as a child-minder, your workplace is likely to be a family home and you are unlikely to be working as a member of a team.

NANNY

Many young people on child-care courses consider the job option of nannying. As a nanny you would be expected to provide full care for the children of the family, and often take sole responsibility while the parents work. Occasionally two families will combine resources to employ a nanny. You might particularly enjoy working with newborn babies, and decide to specialize as a maternity nurse who works with a family for a number of weeks and has special responsibility for the newborn baby. You may work with a family and live in their home (residential), or you may be employed on a daily basis.

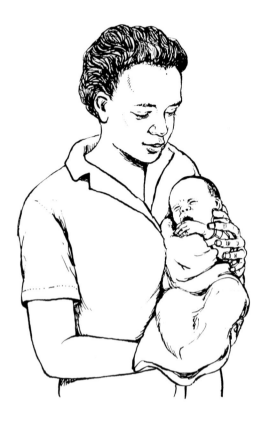

Advantages of residential nannying

- No daily journey to work.
- Possibility of travel with family.
- Money goes further: no rent, fares or food bills.
- Possibility of better communication and contact with the parents.
- Living conditions usually good.
- Possibility of enhanced lifestyle.

Disadvantages of residential nannying

- *Lack of privacy.*
- *May be asked to do more than you should.*
- *May feel guilty if unwell.*
- *Accommodation tied to employment.*
- *May not be treated as part of the family.*
- *May be caught up in the emotional problems of the family.*
- *May not be allowed to entertain friends.*
- *May feel isolated from peers.*

Advantages of daily nannying

■ Control of your own social life.

■ Hours clearly defined, therefore you are less available to be taken advantage of.

■ Easier to change jobs, as you have your own home base.

■ Perceived more as a professional person.

Disadvantages of daily nannying

■ *Money does not go as far.*

■ *Travelling time.*

■ *Communication and liaison with parents can be more difficult.*

After qualifying, working in a private family can offer useful and valuable experience. This can be a comfortable and exhilarating life, but in the long term offers little in the way of career prospects. You may feel isolated from your professional peer group and it can be more difficult to keep in touch with current ideas and good practice while it is important that you keep up your professional knowledge.

It is sensible to work in your home country, gaining experience and skills, before seeking work abroad. Some countries are seen to be more dangerous to women on their own than others, so do seek advice and try and learn the language of the country. America is one place where you will know the language, and there are reputable organizations that will employ you, such as Au Pair America.

If wishing to work outside the European Union countries you must investigate whether you need a work permit; you will almost certainly need a visa. It is the intention of the EU that all professional and educational qualifications will eventually become acceptable in any member state, so it should become increasingly straightforward to obtain work in Europe.

Make sure that wherever you go, you have enlisted the aid of a reputable agency, and that you have sufficient money for emergencies and a return flight.

Advantages of being a nanny
- Working in a safe comfortable environment, with a pleasant family, and with perhaps the opportunity for travel.
- Working in a close relationship with a small number of children.
- Making decisions and using your own initiative.
- The chance to socialize with other nannies.
- Opportunities to meet a variety of different people through the parents.

Disadvantages of being a nanny
- *The possibility of feeling isolated.*
- *Parents possibly not understanding your role.*
- *Possible conflicts (with the parents) over child-rearing practice, conditions of service or job description.*
- *No training or career development prospects.*
- *Not belonging to a pension scheme.*

MOTHER'S HELP

Before you start your child-care training, you might like some experience of working in a family. As an untrained person, you would be expected to do some housework for all the family, not just the children, and even if called a nanny, you would be a mother's help. Sometimes the term 'au pair' is loosely applied to this kind of employment.

CHILD-MINDER

Anyone caring for children under eight years in their own home for payment for more than two hours in any day must register as a child-minder, unless the child is a close blood relative. This is a growing area of employment, with more and more mothers requiring child-minding services so they can return to work after taking maternity leave.

If you wish to be a registered child-minder, you must apply to Ofsted. There are two types of register, the Early Years Register and the Childcare Register.

The Early Years Register

All child-carers providing for children from birth to the 31 August following their fifth birthday, including child-minders, day nurseries, pre-schools and private nursery schools – must register on the **Early Years Register** and deliver the **Early Years Foundation Stage** (EYFS). This is a curriculum framework. If you have undertaken a child-care course, you will already be familiar with it. If not, you will find out about it on the pre-registration briefings and the introductory child-minding course, which child-minders are required to attend as part of the registration process. Providers delivering the curriculum will be registered and inspected against the requirements of the EYFS by Ofsted.

Childcare Register

This is a register of providers who are registered by Ofsted to care for children from birth to 17 years. The register has two parts:

- **the voluntary part**

  Providers who are not eligible for compulsory registration may choose to register here. These are mainly people looking after children aged eight and over, or providing care in the child's home (including nannies).
- **the compulsory part**

  Providers must register if they care for one or more children following their fifth birthdays until they reach their eighth birthdays.

More information about registration on the Childcare Register is available online at www.ofsted.gov.uk. Settings to which the EYFS applies must also meet the Early Years Foundation Stage welfare requirements. These fall into the following five categories:

- Safeguarding and promoting children's welfare.
- Suitable people.
- Suitable premises, environment and equipment.
- Organization.
- Documentation.

During registration and during subsequent inspections, an Ofsted Inspector will evaluate how you meet the welfare requirements. Child-minders are expected to demonstrate the safety and suitability of the domestic premises, inside and outside.

One child-minder can care for:

- up to six children under eight years
- of these six, usually no more than three children can be under five years

- of the three under five years, usually no more than one child can be under a year.

These figures include the child-minder's own children. Exceptions can be made for multiple births and siblings. Child-carers who demonstrate that they can meet and reconcile the varying needs of all the children they care for may be able to care for two babies under one year. This choice of career often appeals to more mature people who have children of their own and accommodation which has enough room for several children.

Advantages

- A useful way of earning money while remaining at home and of gaining experience of children with different needs and ages.
- Flexible job, where you can set your own hours.
- Providing companionship for your own children.
- Possible access to some training programmes offered by your local authority, and can lead to training for a professional qualification.
- Providing interim employment for you while your children are young, before you seek work outside the home.

Disadvantages

- Possible poor pay and long hours.
- Possible interference with your family's social life.
- Possible wear and tear on your home and furniture.
- Some families perhaps finding it difficult to pay or be unwilling to do so if they go on holiday, and it can be embarrassing to chase defaulters.
- Possible sense of isolation and a lack of adult company.
- Not being a part of any career pattern, and there may be little motivation to keep up to date with current good practice.
- Possibly needing to purchase a number of expensive safety items of equipment.
- Possibly having to deal with difficult parents without support.

For further advice, help and information, visit the National Childminding Association (NCMA) at www.ncma.org.uk.

Activity

Working as a nanny and as a child-minder both involve a close relationship with parents, and may present problems. How would these differ in each job?

A team meeting

Working in a team

You may prefer to work as part of a team in an establishment or as part of an organization such as a mainstream or special needs educational establishment, a day-care centre, pre-school, crèche or hospital.

EDUCATION

Many qualified child-care practitioners, searching for their first job, will try for a position in a school. This will most often be working with pre-school children, in a nursery class or a nursery school, either within the state system or in an independent school. Some local authorities employ qualified child-care practitioners in nursery, infant and primary schools to work with children from three to seven years. Working in a school appeals particularly to parents of school-age children, as the holidays and the hours are compatible.

In a school you will be part of a multi-disciplinary team usually headed by a teacher. There are limited career opportunities in an educational post but a great deal of experience is gained working in an establishment as part of a team, and this will stand you in very good stead in any later career that you might choose. The practice that you will contribute to in a school is usually of a high standard, with the emphasis on the cognitive development of the child. You will be expected to contribute to the curriculum planning and to the team, to do observations and make assessments, and to liaise with parents.

Nursery schools may be part of the local authority provision and may be secular or belong to a particular faith; they may be owned privately by individuals, or even jointly owned by state and voluntary bodies. The child-care practitioner interested in the Montessori method may seek employment in a Montessori school. In a state school, your pay and conditions of service will be tightly regulated and will be the same as anyone else in a similar job with similar experience in your local authority. In the private sector, salary and conditions vary from school to school.

Educational establishments are interested in providing regular in-service training for staff, and you will need to inquire what your school will provide for you.

Advantages
- Shorter hours, longer holidays.
- Well-structured multi-disciplinary team, offering good practical experience and companionship, with recognition of skills.
- Access to in-service training.

Disadvantages
- *Lack of promotion and career path, reflected in the scarcity of men entering the profession.*
- *Pay difficult to live on for someone living on his or her own.*
- *Occasionally, lack of respect for professional qualification.*
- *Sometimes, lack of leadership and no recognition of the professional skills of the child-care practitioner, can lead to rigid working practices and lack of motivation to progress.*

SPECIAL NEEDS EDUCATION

Many children with special needs are educated in mainstream schools, but those with more severe disabilities may be educated in special schools. Child-care practitioners are employed as part of a multi-disciplinary team, which will include teachers, physiotherapists, speech therapists, social workers and medical professionals. Your role in a special school may involve caring for children whose stage of development is below their chronological age. As well as contributing to the curriculum, you will be expected to understand and meet the children's physical needs. In some circumstances, you may be involved in lifting and moving children. Training will be given for this.

There are schools for children with physical disabilities, such as hearing and vision impairment, and for children with cerebral palsy. There are educational establishments for children with learning difficulties and for those with emotional and behavioural needs. Caring for and educating children with special needs is often physically tiring and emotionally stressful, but offers a great deal of fulfilment and job satisfaction. This type of employment gives child-care practitioners more responsibility than many other jobs in education.

Advantages and disadvantages

Similar to any job in education, except that you may be valued more for your qualification and skills, and the specialist knowledge that you gain may well be advantageous in seeking future employment.

DAY CARE

Day care encompasses care provided for children of working parents and care provided by social services for families where some professional support is required. Day care differs from education in that children may attend from a very young age and the day offered may start as early as seven-thirty in the morning and finish at six o'clock in the evening. In some workplace nurseries the hours may be extended beyond this time.

There are several types of day care:

- social services nurseries, such as family centres and day nurseries, provided by the local authority
- workplace provision, provided by the employer
- community nurseries, possibly set up by parents with grant aid
- franchised nurseries, run by companies to a certain standard
- private nurseries
- university and college nurseries
- voluntary sector nurseries, often run by charities such as Save the Children.

Day-care settings are registered by Ofsted and deliver the EYFS.

Advantages

- Higher salary.
- More responsibility and opportunities for promotion within a career structure.
- On-going training for people in social services nurseries, and many of the others.
- Closer partnership with parents.
- Recognition of professional qualification.
- Liaising with other professionals.

Disadvantages

- Longer hours and shorter holidays.
- More meetings and administration that may take you away from your work with children.
- Possible stress caused by working with parents and families who are experiencing difficulties.
- In some centres, the uncertainty of grants and funding may add to stress, and need to be addressed by fund-raising.

CHILDREN'S CENTRES

Children's Centres offer a range of services for children and families under one roof, giving staff the opportunity to work in a multi-disciplinary team. This may include Early Years practitioners and workers from the health and social care sectors, such as health visitors, speech and language therapists and social workers.

Sure Start is the government's programme to deliver the best start in life for every child by bringing together early education, child-care, health and family support. Some Sure Start initiatives apply universally, while others only apply in targeted local areas and/or to disadvantaged groups in England.

Responsibility for Sure Start lies with The Early Years, Extended Schools and Special Needs Group, which belongs to the Department for Children, Schools and Families. Sure Start tells us the following about their service:

Services

- Sure Start covers children from conception through to age 14, and up to age 16 for those with special educational needs and disabilities. It also aims to help parents and communities across the country.
- There are a wide range of services currently available, from Children's Centres and early support programmes to information and advice on health and financial matters. We are helping set and maintain childcare standards.
- Sure Start is the cornerstone of the Government's drive to tackle child poverty and social exclusion working with parents-to-be, parents/carers and children to promote the physical, intellectual and social development of babies and young children so that they can flourish at home and when they get to school.
- All Sure Start local programmes have become children's centres. Local authorities are responsible for Sure Start children's centres, and the services on offer may vary from area to area.

How do our services work?

Our services bring together universal, free, early education and more and better childcare. Sure Start does this with greater support where there is greater need through children's tax credit, children's centres and Sure Start local programmes.

Integrated Early Years Services

For some time we have been encouraging the delivery of childcare alongside early education and other health and family services.

Sure Start Children's Centres

Sure Start Children's Centres are building on existing successful initiatives like Sure Start Local Programmes, Neighbourhood Nurseries and Early Excellence Centres, and bringing high-quality integrated early years services to the heart of communities.

Our target of 2,500 children's centres was reached in early March 2008, and 2,914 centres have now been established (October 2008), offering services to over 2.3 million young children and their families.

By 2010, the number of children's centres will increase to 3,500 – so every family has easy access to high-quality integrated services in their community and the benefits of Sure Start can be felt nationwide.

Early Education

All 3- and 4-year-olds are now guaranteed a free, part-time (12½ hours per week, 38 weeks per year, increasing to 15 hours per week in 2010), early-education place. There are over 37,000 settings delivering free, Government-funded, early education in the maintained, private, voluntary and independent sectors.

Childcare

In June 2008, the stock of registered childcare stood at approaching 1.3 million places (more than double the 1997 level).

There will be a childcare place for all children aged between 3 and 14, between the hours of 8am and 6pm each weekday by 2010, when there will be over 2 million sustainable childcare places for children up to 14.

PRE-SCHOOLS

These may be run by the Pre-school Learning Alliance (formerly PPA), local authorities or by groups of parents frustrated by lack of local provision. They are run on a sessional basis, often for half a day, although some may run all day. Parents frequently help on a rota basis, and often are involved in the management. The emphasis is on play and social interaction, and the age range is from two to five years.

Child-care practitioners are employed to organize the groups, enriching them by their specialist knowledge. Pre-schools are registered by Ofsted and deliver the EYFS. The regulations that apply to day-care settings also apply to pre-schools.

Advantages
- Short day and long holidays. This job may well suit a parent with his or her own pre-school child.
- Opportunities to meet local parents, so that your own social network enlarges.
- Less formal than most educational and day-care establishments.
- Satisfaction in sharing knowledge with parents.

Disadvantages
- *Low pay.*
- *Uncertainty of funding.*
- *Frequently having to share premises, which involves setting up and tidying away all the equipment at the beginning and end of each session.*
- *Procedures for complaints and grievances are sometimes unclear.*
- *Limited career development.*

CRÈCHES

There is a growing area of work for child-care practitioners in crèches set up in supermarkets, clinics, hospitals, airports, sports and leisure centres and shopping centres, where parents can leave their children with qualified staff for a short period of time. You will work with children from babyhood through to primary age.

The work is varied, as some days you may have very few children, and others you will have up to the capacity allowed. You may not be able to predict the age of the children that you will be asked to care for, and the job demands flexibility, organizational skills and initiative.

The growth in world-wide leisure and tourism has resulted in opportunities for working abroad, such as in tour operator's holiday facilities, crèches on luxury liners, and in summer camps at home and abroad.

Advantages
- Flexible hours.
- Variety of experience, no two days are the same.

Disadvantages
- *Shift work, where some hours may not suit you.*
- *Not getting to know the children and establish long-term relationships.*
- *No prior knowledge of parents and children.*
- *Limited career development.*

HOSPITALS

Opportunities for working in hospitals can occur in either the National Health Service or in the private sector. You might be employed in a unit caring for newborn babies, either on the post-natal ward or in the special-care baby unit. The paediatric wards of large hospitals may house hospital schools or provide playworkers for children. Some hospitals have special assessment units, where the observation skills and the understanding of developmental needs of children by the child-care practitioner is especially valued.

Currently, the National Health Service appears to be encouraging more nursery nurses to work alongside other health professionals, such as health visitors in health centres, and in children's wards in hospitals.

Advantages
- Further training may be available.
- Acquisition of new skills.
- Flexible hours.
- Working in a large multi-disciplinary team.
- Social atmosphere of working in a large establishment.

Disadvantages
- *Long days and unsocial hours.*
- *Lack of promotion and career development.*
- *Having to deal with the bureaucracy of a large establishment.*
- *The stress of working with sick and terminally ill children.*
- *Low salary.*

Working part-time

Not everyone is looking for a full-time job. It might suit you to start your employment career either by seeking a permanent part-time post, or working on a temporary or casual basis, either through an agency or becoming part of a 'bank' of workers, or to hold a permanent full-time post which you share with another person. If you decide to 'job share' you will receive pay and benefits in proportion to the part of the job you do.

Advantages
- More time to give to other responsibilities, such as family.
- Time to devote to new hobbies, interests or part-time courses.
- Shorter hours.

Disadvantages
- *Restriction in the choice and availability of work.*
- *Poor career structure.*
- *Possible communication problems with the person you are sharing the job with, particularly if there is no time overlap.*

Other areas of employment

It is still possible to gain employment in residential homes, particularly those for children with special needs, although current policy dictates that as many children as possible should be supported in their own homes or fostered. Child-care practitioners can also find work in out-of-school clubs (caring for school aged children before school, after school and in the holidays within a play setting), where their skills, being similar to those of playworkers, are highly valued. As more day-care settings (such as private nurseries) and schools open their own clubs, it is increasingly common for Early Years or education workers to also work in a play setting during the course of a normal working day. A position in an out-of-school club often suits pre-school workers who want to work full-time hours, as the pre-school will be open for school hours during term-time only, and the out-of-school club will only open when schools are closed.

The main qualification for an educational home visitor, who visits very young children in their own homes, is to be a parent. The educational home visitor's role is to help parents to understand how play helps learning, and to be interactive with their children. If you have a child-care qualification you will be well suited for this valuable but part-time work, although formal qualifications are not always sought.

As with every other profession, employment opportunities are constantly changing and evolving. An example of this is the recent development where qualified nursery nurses work alongside health visitors in clinics and in health centres. Some local authorities are now employing child-care practitioners in respite schemes, set up to allow families a break from caring for children with special needs. Sometimes the respite extends to single parents, so that they can have some time to themselves.

There are people who feel they need to experience many different types of work before settling into a long-term commitment. This skill mix is becoming more popular and there appears to be a trend in urban areas to register with an agency shortly after qualifying, to gain a variety of different employment experiences.

As can be seen, some jobs offer more opportunities in career development terms and in-service training and promotion, while others might offer longer holidays or higher salaries.

Assessing your own needs

The table on page 16 will allow you to think through your needs and priorities in employment. Tick the aspects that are important to you in the top set of boxes. When considering different types of employment, check the opportunities outlined on the chart against your own needs. You will be able to do this using the job description and conditions of service sent to you with each application form, supplemented by asking questions at interview.

Activity
Discuss the reasons why child care is sometimes regarded as a low-status occupation. How could you, as an individual and as a member of a professional organization, challenge this perception?

Further reading

Moss P. and Penn H., *Transforming Nursery Education*, Paul Chapman, 1996
Reuvid, J., *Working Abroad: The Complete Guide to Overseas Employment*, Kogan Page Ltd, 2008
Stacey, M., *Teamwork and Collaboration in Early Years Settings*, Learning Network, 2009

What do you want from employment?

	Travel				Crèches			Hospitals				Day care										Education						In the home		
	Working abroad as nanny	Working abroad for tour operator	Summer camps	Ships	Supermarkets	Sports & leisure centres	Shopping centres	Obstetric	Paediatric	Assessment centres	Health centres/clinics	Social services	Community	Voluntary	Workplace	Private	Franchised	Residential	University/College	Pre-School	Out-of-school care	Nursery	Primary or Infant School	Private	State	Special needs	Educational home visiting	Daily nanny	Residential nanny	Child-minder
Full-time hours																														
Part-time hours																														
Flexible hours																														
Shift work																														
Good salary																														
Promotion prospects																														
In-service training																														
Opportunity to gain further qualifications																														
Residential work																														
Long holidays																														
Sole responsibility																														
Working in a team																														
Variety																														
Travel																														
Opportunity to use initiative																														
Social activities																														
Low stress factor																														
Opportunity to use observation skills																														
Opportunity to use specific skills & talents																														
Job security																														
Short journey to work																														

2 JOB SEARCH

The process of finding a job can be long and demanding, so it is best to start looking in good time. If you are on a course, which finishes in July, it would not be too early to start the process in May.

If you are looking for a post as a nanny, the main ways of approaching this would be to go to a reputable agency in your area, or to look in specialist magazines, such as *Nursery World* or *The Lady*. Sometimes advertisements are carried in daily or local papers. The safest approach is obviously through an agency, as they should also have interviewed the family.

Agencies

Anyone can register with a private employment agency to look for work. There are many that specialize in child-care employment, offering both permanent and temporary vacancies. The agency may put you in touch with a prospective employer, or may employ you themselves to work in a variety of different settings.

Agencies will require information from you relating to your qualifications, past experiences, skills and personal details, and will request names of referees. They are not allowed by law to charge a fee to the job seeker. It is the employer who pays the agency for filling the post.

Answering individual advertisements

If you apply through a newspaper advertisement or a postcard advertisement in a newsagent's window or on a college notice board, you should be aware of the risks involved. If you set up an interview in this way, you should, at the very least, let someone know where you are going, and who

you are going to see. It is safer still to take someone with you. In this situation there is likely to be apprehension on both sides, as parents may be reluctant to have someone waiting in another room while they interview a prospective nanny, so your friend should be prepared to wait outside the house. This is a sad reflection of our times.

After your first job, it is quite likely that you will hear of other posts through personal contacts and recommendations, and this will do a great deal to allay any fears you may have in approaching new families.

Professional journals and newspapers

You will find nanny jobs advertised in professional journals, magazines, and in local papers. These may also carry a risk and care should be taken to protect yourself.

Jobs in day care, hospitals and education are advertised at a professional level, and ensure equality of opportunity. They will be advertised in national and local newspapers, and in specialist magazines. If you make a personal approach to a local social services department, health authority or education authority, you would be informed of current vacancies and where they are advertised.

Public Services positions are also advertised in one place online, at http://jobseekers.direct.gov.uk. You can use the search facility to find jobs in your local area.

The papers and journals will carry advertisements for a wide range of different child-care employment opportunities. Many publications also place their job advertisements on their websites. A good advertisement will tell you about the organization or family, the job itself and something of the qualities of the applicant required by the employer.

You may be asked to respond in different ways:

- by making telephone contact
- sending a handwritten letter of application
- sending a simple letter requesting details of the post
- sending a curriculum vitae (c.v.). It is important that you respond as requested in the advertisement.

Your local job centre will advertise positions and also offer advice and support for jobseekers. These services can also be found online at www.jobcentreplus.gov.uk. You can use the search facility to find jobs in your local area. (Not all employers advertise their positions with the job centre, so be sure to also look in local newspapers and professional journals.)

Every local authority also offers career information and advice to young people through a Connexions Direct service. To find out what services are available in your area, visit www.connexions-direct.com.

Activity
Look at four different copies of *Nursery World*. Identify the range of job opportunities and the appropriate way to reply.

Job-hunting techniques

It is useful to keep a record of your job applications, listing each job you apply for, the date of application, the interview date and the response. It is helpful to try and assess why you were successful, or not, and if the job for which you had applied was right for you. This information will be useful in future job applications.

Always keep documentation in a secure place, retaining copies of the application form, the advertisement and any information sent to you by the organization, so that you may refer to it before the interview. It is likely you will apply for a number of posts as you finish your training, and keeping a child-care job search record will help you to be clear about the progress of each application. If you are not offered employment, the reasons why may emerge from this record, particularly in your comments.

Child-care job search record

	1	2	3	4
Job title				
Employer's name & address Tel no.				
Type of establishment Age range				
Where advertised Date seen Closing date				
Type of response Date				
Details received Date				
Completed application returned date				
Copy taken				
Date application acknowledged				
Result Date				
Interview Date				
Outcome and date				
Comments				

This page may be photocopied. © Nelson Thornes Ltd.

Child-care job search record

	1	2	3	4
Job title	Nursery Nurse	Nanny	Nursery Nurse	
Employer's name & address Tel no.	Holby Hospital Bristol BS12 8QT	7 Hill View Bristol Avon	High Rise Nursery School	
Type of establishment Age range	Paediatric Unit 0-16 yrs	Private family 4/12 2yrs. 7 yrs	Nursery School 3-5 yrs	
Where advertised Date seen Closing date	Nursery World 1.9.09 30.9.09	Avon Evening News 3.9.09 not given	Nursery World 1.9.09 6.10.09	
Type of response Date	Letter of application 3.9.09	phone call 4.9.09	Letter of application & CV. 6.9.09	
Details received Date	Job description Application form Person specification 6.9.09	details given on phone 4.9.09	Job Descrip = ops policy. Persn spec appli. form school news-letter 13.9.09	
Completed application returned date	15.9.09	N/A	20.9.09	
Copy taken	✓		✓	
Date application acknowledged	20.9.09		28.9.09	
Result Date	Interview 6.10.09		Interview 12.10.09	
Interview Date	✓ 12.10.09	8.9.09	✓ 14.10.09	
Outcome and date	Not offered post	Offered post 10.9.09	Offered post 18.10.09	
Comments	10 people interviewed. Many more experienced. Dried up in interview Could not think of questions I had prepared to ask	Did not accept. Did not feel comfortable with parents. Unrealistic expectations	Accepted	

In your first job you may not gain employment with the age group you prefer, or in the type of establishment where you would like your career to develop. Rather than wait for the perfect job to come along, why not register with an agency to gain a wide range of experience? You might discover you are better suited to a type of work you had not previously considered, and when the job you want comes along, you will be in a better position to apply for it. You may wish to approach key organizations yourself, perhaps sending a speculative letter, or making a telephone call.

You may have very definite ideas about your career development, and have a plan for your working life or you may be more flexible, wanting to try different jobs in the child-care area and see where they may lead. Both these approaches are perfectly valid and depend upon your personality and what suits you individually.

Further reading

Greenwood, D., *The Job Hunter's Handbook*, Kogan Page Ltd, 1999

Parkinson, M., *Your Job Search Made Easy*, 3rd Edition, Kogan Page Ltd, 2002

Sonnenblick, C., *Job Hunting Made Easy*, Learning Express, 1997

3 APPLYING FOR EMPLOYMENT

Applying for any employment requires careful planning, preparation and organization. You will need to understand the stages and sequence of the application process, and approach it with the same enthusiasm and professional skills as you do in all your work.

What you have to offer

It is a very valuable exercise, before beginning the process of applying for a job, to consider your strengths, and evaluate what you have to offer.

The table on pages 24–25 contains the main attributes required of any successful child-care practitioner. Some of these attributes may figure more prominently in some types of employment, for example, it is very necessary to be able to cope well with frequent and unexpected changes if you are applying for a job with an agency. If you have a low score in this area, you may be better suited to apply for a job that is more predictable.

Preparing your curriculum vitae (c.v.)

Your 'curriculum vitae' is a summary of your career. This Latin phrase meaning 'the course of life' has come to mean that area of your life that you have spent in employment, and an outline of other experiences and interests that may be regarded as relevant by a potential employer.

If you have access to a word processor, you will find it easier to tailor your c.v. to each specific job you are applying for. While being totally

SELF-APPRAISAL BEFORE EMPLOYMENT	ASSESSMENT OF ABILITY low medium high			Did you enjoy the placement?	In this area were your placement reports Poor/Satisfactory/Good?
Relationships and ability to work with:					
babies 0–1 years					
children 1–3 years					
children 3–5 years					
children 5–8 years					
children 8–12 years					
children 13–16 years					
colleagues in placements					
parents in placements					
peer group					
college tutors/line managers					
Understanding of children's needs and development:					
physical					
cognitive					
language					
social					
emotional					
moral					
spiritual/aesthetic					
Experience with:					
a family					
children in a multicultural environment					
gifted children					
children with special needs					
children in a hospital unit					
children in day care					
children in out-of-school care					
children in education					

SELF-APPRAISAL BEFORE EMPLOYMENT *(continued)*	ASSESSMENT OF ABILITY			Did you enjoy the placement?	In this area were your placement reports Poor/Satisfactory/Good?
	low	medium	high		
Professional skills:					
regular attendance					
punctual					
commitment to equal opportunities					
good team member					
Communication skills:					
writing reports, observations etc.					
listening and oral skills					
presentation of self					
Personality profile:					
sense of humour					
flexibility					
cheerfulness					
enthusiasm					
leadership					
outgoing					
ability to take direction					
responsiveness to constructive criticism					
maturity					
staying power					
initiative					
Do you prefer working with large groups of children?					
Do you prefer individual work with children?					

honest, you should emphasize the particular strengths and experiences required by the post. Remember that you may well be asked to elaborate on any area of your c.v. at interview.

POINTS TO REMEMBER

- The c.v. should be typed, and presented tidily on white A4 paper.
- Some people think that an imaginative and unusual presentation will have more impact. It may, but it could put as many people off as it interests. Ask friends, colleagues or tutors for their response.
- Spelling and grammar must be correct (have it checked).
- Keep it brief. It should be no more than two pages long.
- Avoid solid blocks of script.
- Use space to emphasize points and make sections stand out.
- Get a tutor or friend to check it for any ambiguity. It may be clear to you but muddled to an outsider.
- Update it regularly.

Your basic c.v. should include:
- personal details
- education and qualifications
- work experience and career history
- personal interests and hobbies
- other relevant details.

PERSONAL DETAILS

These should include your name, address to which you wish correspondence to be sent, telephone numbers, gender and date of birth. Some application forms might ask for your nationality, your marital status and whether you have dependent children, but it is not necessary to include this information on your c.v.

EDUCATION AND QUALIFICATIONS

Start with the highest qualification. If you have a degree, it will be presumed that you have A levels and GCSEs, so only list these if you are specifically asked to on your application form. Make sure that you list your qualifications clearly, spacing them well apart. It is not necessary to include any failures unless there is a large time gap on your c.v. If you did not finish a course, put 'course discontinued'. If you failed a course, you may wish to explain briefly why. If you have overseas qualifications, it is

Curriculum Vitae

Sally Smith

22 Albert Street
Bristol
BS22 8DL
Telephone no: 01722 12345

Date of Birth: 23 March 1990

I am a responsible and confident team worker who has experience in working with children aged 0–8 years. I am looking for a position in a Hospital setting.

PERSONAL STRENGTHS

I am:
• Enthusiastic and highly motivated.
• Able to work under pressure.
• Extremely patient.

I have:
• Excellent communication skills.
• An in-depth knowledge of children's development.

EDUCATION AND QUALIFICATIONS

School

John Ruskin School
Pride Street
Bristol
BS22 7PQ

GCSE Results

C – English Language
C – English Literature
C – Design and Communication
C – Art and Design

I attended the school from 2001–2006

College

Tamworth College of FE
Wellington Road
Bristol
BS22 6AB

Qualifications

BTEC National Diploma in
Children's Care,
Learning and Development,

First Aid Certificate – St John's Ambulance

I attended the college from 2006–2008

During this time I successfully completed work placements in four different child-care settings, ranging from 0–8 years.

WORK EXPERIENCE

Sainsbury plc
Weston Green
Bristol
Avon

I worked as a Saturday Sales Assistant. My duties included: serving the customers, using a computerised till, handling customers' complaints.

I worked there from December 2006–October 2008

(continued)

Prior Hope Nursery School Weston High, Bristol BS22 9AC	Ages: 3–5 year olds My duties included: • Carrying out activities with the children • Working in a team

I attended there: September 2006–July 2007

Templeton Primary School Templeton Row Bristol BS22 1SOA	Ages: 5–7 year olds My duties included: • Working with the children • Working in a team with the other staff • Completing activities with the children • Contributing to the National Curriculum

I attended there: September 2007–January 2008

Holby Hospital Bristol BS12 8QT	Ages: Newborn–2–3 weeks My duties included: • Caring for the babies • Demonstrating bathing, top and tailing • Working with the parents • Observation in SCBU

I spent two weeks there in the month of January 2008

St Francis Community Nursery Weston Green Bristol BS15 0AT	Ages: 6 months–4 years My duties included: • Working in a team • Planning activities, implementing them and completing written work • Stimulating the children

I attended there: February 2008–present time
I currently run a weekly crèche for St. Francis Community Nursery

INTERESTS

In my spare time I enjoy swimming and going to aerobics sessions, I also enjoy going to karate lessons.

I like to read novels and non-fiction. History books interest me because I would like to increase my knowledge of how other people lived.

In the future I would like to travel and maybe settle in a foreign country, where I would continue my career in a child-care setting.

REFEREES

Cynthia Johns (Academic)
Tamworth College of FE
Wellington Road
Bristol BS22 6AB

Rev Charles Duckworth
St Francis Community Nursery
Weston Green
Bristol
BS15 0AT

advisable to note their equivalent UK level. If you have been on any relevant training programmes, you might feel it a good idea to list them. First aid and food handler's certificates would be appropriate.

WORK EXPERIENCE AND CAREER HISTORY

Start with your most recent job, because if your prospective employer has many applications to read, he or she will probably just skim through your c.v., and the last job should be the most relevant. Each employment needs to be clearly separated, with the month as well as the year. You should include full-time, vacation and part-time work, both paid and voluntary. It is unnecessary to give addresses of your past employers, but you should include the dates of employment, job title, and duties and responsibilities undertaken. Explain any gaps in your employment. For younger students, details of your work experience either in school or college should be stated in this section.

It is important to match the description of your experience to the job you are applying for. Describe briefly what you did in each post, and note any achievements or successes. Remember that only you can outline your skills, so you do not need to be modest. Be brief and to the point. This is the most important part of your c.v., so work on it and get advice. Avoid jargon and convoluted sentences.

PERSONAL INTERESTS AND HOBBIES

This should be a fairly short section of the c.v., perhaps more useful for the younger person who has not yet had the opportunity to develop a career. You need to show yourself in the best possible light, so only list those hobbies which make you look interesting, active and enthusiastic, and which might be of use in the prospective job. Any interest showing team involvement or initiative would be useful to list. Indicate in some hobbies whether you watch or participate: just putting 'cricket', for instance, would not be enough. It is not a good idea to mention politics or religion.

OTHER RELEVANT DETAILS

Use your discretion. These might include a driving licence, the fact that you do not smoke, knowledge of other languages, a swimming or life-saving certificate and computer skills. Membership of any professional organization, such as the Professional Association of Nursery Nurses, should be included here.

A c.v. usually ends with the names and addresses of two people who would be willing to write a reference for you. You should quote their occupation or job title. Always ask their permission before giving their names.

Covering and accompanying letters

Most employers, when asking you to fill in an application form, will also require a covering letter. This should be handwritten, neat, well spaced and using conventional letter writing techniques. If your skills in this direction are not of the highest, you will find several books in your library putting you on the right path. The type of paper you use and the neatness of your handwriting will convey an impression of your personality and educational achievement.

22 Albert St
Bristol
BS22 9PQ

23.05.09

The Personnel Officer
Holby Hospital
Bristol
BS12 8Q2

Dear Sir/Madam

I am writing to you to apply for the position of nursery worker, which I saw advertised in the Western Daily Post.

After leaving school with four GCSEs A–C grades, I immediately enrolled at college on to the BTEC National Diploma in Children's Care, Learning and Development, while I was there we studied Child Health, Child Development and Social studies.

I am keen to start my career working in the Hospital sector where I would like to achieve my goal of working with young babies.

As you will see from my c.v. I successfully completed two weeks of work experience at Holby Hospital, where I worked with nursery nurses in caring for the babies. I demonstrated bathing and top and tailing to the new parents. I really enjoy working with babies and I feel that this is where my strengths lie. I work well in a team and can work well under pressure. I am flexible, enthusiastic and highly motivated.

I believe that I would be an asset to you and a valuable member of staff within your highly prestigious Hospital. I am available for interview at any time and look forward to hearing from you soon.

Yours faithfully
Sally Smith

An example of an accompanying letter

The letter falls into three sections:

- who you are, and why you are writing
- what you are offering
- what you hope to get in reply to your letter.

It should be brief and to the point. It should indicate the job you are applying for and quote any reference number. You should show you understand what the job involves and that you have some knowledge of the age group and type of establishment. Give your reasons for applying for the post and guide the employer where to look for the most important information on your c.v. Target your skills and achievements to the job requirements, state why you feel you are suitable for this post and what you are offering them rather than what you expect to gain. Say when you are available for interview. The letter should show interest and enthusiasm.

Speculative letters

These are sent to prospective employers stating what type of post you are interested in, asking if there are any vacancies, and outlining your qualifications and experience. A c.v. could be enclosed, and you should follow up your enquiry with a telephone call, usually after three to five working days.

Activity
Choose an area of work that particularly interests you. Write a speculative letter to the person in charge. Having completed the exercise, compare your letter with others in your group.

Telephone techniques

You may be asked in an advertisement to make telephone contact with a named person. Give yourself time when doing this and make sure you are not going to be interrupted. Try to use a private phone rather than a pay phone, and have the advertisement by you when you ring. Speak slowly and clearly, stating where you saw the advertisement, your reason for interest in the job, and your name and full address, including the post code. If you are applying for a job as a nanny (or even, perhaps, for a job with a small private school), the telephone conversation might turn into a short-listing interview, so make sure that you have your c.v. with you, so that you can answer any questions clearly and concisely as to your qualifications and previous experience. You may wish to make some notes yourself, so have a pencil and some paper available.

Once you have made your first approach, you will be sent an application form, a job description, the person specification and possibly information concerning the establishment and details of any equal opportunity policy. All documentation should be read carefully and thoroughly before you put pen to paper. It is rare to be sent information concerning the conditions of service, but you should be given this information at interview, in the form of a contract if you are successful.

The application

An example of an application form can be seen at www.ealing.gov.uk/services/jobs/how_to_apply/index.html. There may well be instructions enclosed with the form as to how to fill it in, and you must read these carefully. You may be asked not to send a c.v. as the form will extract all the relevant information. The first thing to do is to photocopy the form, so that you can initially fill in a draft. Read all the other literature, so that you make appropriate responses. Answer all the questions on the form, and use black ink, so that it can be photocopied clearly. They are confidential documents so you need not be reticent.

There will be sections under the following headings:

- personal details
- employment history
- education and training

- membership of professional organizations
- medical information
- disclosure of any criminal convictions (as you will be in regular contact with children you are not exempt from the Rehabilitation of Offenders Act, 1974)
- monitoring information concerning race, gender and disability.

The first four items are likely to be the same as information held on your c.v. You are obliged to disclose any medical information as honestly as possible, and this holds true for the disclosure of any criminal convictions. The employer will verify this information with referees and will carry out a police check. The information required for monitoring is to ensure that equal opportunities policies are working properly.

Activity
Describe three ways in which an employer might discriminate against certain groups of people when recruiting personnel.

The part of the form that you will have to think about very carefully is the section where you will be asked to describe your relevant skills and experience, and what you think you can bring to the job. You need to read, with care, the job description and the person specification (see examples of these on pages 34–39) so that you can match your knowledge, your personality, your attitudes, your skills and your interests with the job. All areas must be fully answered. A well-constructed and completed form should be enough to grant you an interview. This is the only method there is of judging which applicants meet the criteria for short-listing.

You will be required to provide the names and addresses of two referees, one of whom will be your last or present employer. You should be able to request that this reference is not taken up before you are interviewed and offered the post. If you have not yet been in employment, you may give the name of your college tutor. If you have had a particularly successful placement, your supervisor may be happy to write you a reference. You should confirm with the other referee that he or she is prepared to write a reference for you.

When you have finally completed the application form carefully, tidily, and without correction fluid or crossing out, take a photocopy before sending it off. You will be questioned on your answers and it is advisable to take the copy with you if you are offered an interview.

Person specification

NURSERY NURSE

Essential requirements
1 The ability to work with and contribute to the Early Years team, to create an environment which fosters the all-round development of the child.
2 The ability to share responsibility with the class teacher for the planning of an appropriate and stimulating EYFS curriculum.
3 The ability to work closely with class teachers to ensure continuity through the education in the Early Years in order to foster the child's growth, independence and autonomy.
4 The ability to contribute to the regular systems of observations, assessment and record keeping.

Qualifications and experience
1 Applicants must hold a Level 3 child-care and education qualification.
2 Relevant recent experience of working with young children in an education setting is required.

Skills, knowledge and attitudes
1 Applicants should be able to demonstrate an understanding of child development and the Early Years Foundation Stage, and be able to implement this knowledge through their daily practice.
2 Applicants must be able to work as a member of a team (and to express their thoughts and ideas, both orally and in written form).
3 Applicants must display an interest in working with children in an urban, multi-cultural environment and an ability to support children's development in English and their home language.
4 Applicants must be in sympathy with the aims of a Church School.
5 Applicants must be willing to support the Equal Opportunities in the school.

BIGBURGH SCHOOL

Bigburgh Road, Hickton, London N1 7BC
Headteacher Mr R.J. Swithin.   Telephone 0181 1213 45110

Job description

NURSERY NURSE (responsible to: Headteacher/Teacher-in-charge)

Duties/responsibilities

1. To create an educational environment in which the children's all-round development is fostered and the EYFS is delivered, by being a responsible team member in preparing the rooms and outside play area.
2. To foster children's intellectual development through the provision of stimulating activities and positive interaction.
3. To foster children's language development, and, where appropriate, encourage the development of home languages.
4. To foster children's social and emotional development, encouraging independence and high self-esteem.
5. To assist in the physical care of young children, including cleaning, toileting and changing them as necessary.
6. To be aware of children's different educational, physical and special needs, and, as a member of the team, to plan for and strive to meet those needs.
7. To maintain high professional standards and levels of care and hygiene.
8. To participate in observing, monitoring, assessing and recording children's activities in order to maintain written records.
9. To foster and develop good relationships with parents/carers and share with them, as appropriate, information about their child's progress and development.
10. To participate in daily discussion concerning immediate issues.
11. To participate in staff meetings, relating to curriculum planning and development, management, administration, professional practice and personal development of staff.
12. To help promote among the children an understanding, an acceptance of one another and their families.
13. To administer simple first aid when necessary.
14. To assist in the preparation and cleaning up of the general activities, encouraging children's participation in these tasks.
15. To organize materials and equipment for use within the class sharing responsibility for its care and maintenance.
16. To share responsibility for display in the school including mounting of children's work.
17. To help promote amongst the children and their families, and within the wider community, the aims of the school.
18. To be fully committed to implementing the equal opportunities policies of the Borough.
19. To be fully committed to implementing all school policies, including Child Protection procedures.

You will be expected to carry out all duties in the context of and in compliance with the Council's equal opportunities policies.

This job description has been agreed in accordance with the Council's establishment control procedure. This procedure will also apply to any subsequent changes or revisions.

Person specification

Job Title: NURSERY OFFICER

Department: SOCIAL SERVICES

Division/Section: CHILDREN AND FAMILIES

Post No:

Hours: 37½

MAJOR RESPONSIBILITIES

Knowledge, skills and abilities

1 To work as a 'keyworker' in a team with other members of staff in order to share and promote good child-care practices.
2 To work with colleagues on the planning and delivery of a high-quality EYFS curriculum.
3 To plan and provide, with colleagues, a range of stimulating, indoor and outdoor activities that are culturally sensitive and designed to meet each child's needs.
4 To provide child care which promotes a good self-image for all children, that is non-racist and non-sexist.
5 To monitor the children's all-round development and progress, keep accurate records and write reports.
6 To provide an inclusive environment and to meet the needs of children with disabilities.
7 To work in partnership with parents, involving them in decision-making and day-to-day activities in the nursery and pre-school.
8 To work with, and share information with colleagues, internally and externally.
9 To ensure a positive recognition of race, culture, language and religion (for children, parents and colleagues).
10 To make immediate decisions in an emergency without reference to senior staff.
11 To support and train students and volunteers on placement in the nursery.
12 A commitment to the Council's equal opportunities policy and to understand and implement the policies in relation to the job description.

Education and experience

The successful candidate will have a Level 4 child-care and education qualification/teaching qualification
OR
a Level 3 child-care education qualification, and a willingness to undertake Level 4 training.
Experience of working with children in a social service or education environment is essential.

Job description

POST TITLE: NURSERY OFFICER
REPORTS TO (TITLE): OFFICER-IN-CHARGE

POST NO:
DEPARTMENT SECTION: SOCIAL SERVICES

MAIN PURPOSE OF JOB

To work in partnership with parents to provide consistent high quality, non-discriminatory child care which meets the needs of each individual child and family and which enables the child to realize his/her full potential and achieve a good self-image.

DUTIES AND RESPONSIBILITIES

Describe each duty in a separate paragraph listing the main or most important duties first.

1. To be responsible as a keyworker for a small group of children designated to you by the officer-in-charge.
2. To develop a trusting and caring relationship with the child and his/her family.
3. To visit new families at home and be responsible for settling in children taking into account their particular needs.
4. To contribute to the planning and delivery of a high-quality EYFS curriculum.
5. To regularly observe and assess children's progress, maintain records and share this information, as appropriate, with parents, and other professionals.
6. To be responsible for the development and implementation of care plans for individual children.
7. To monitor closely all children, in particular those who are on the child protection register, and to report immediately to the officer-in-charge any significant incidents.
8. To treat any information, or matters relating to the work within the nursery as confidential.
9. To prepare reports and contribute to reviews, case conferences and court proceedings as required.
10. To work in partnership with parents, involving them regularly in the work carried out with their child, and in nursery activities.
11. To provide a service which values and respects the race, religion, language and culture of the children and families using the nursery.
12. To plan and provide a range of attractive stimulating activities, indoors and outdoors, designed to meet each child's needs.
13. To welcome children with disabilities, providing special care if appropriate to meet individual children's needs.
14. To operate as a member of the nursery team and to promote sound working relationships both internally and externally.
15. To stand and contribute to staff meetings, room meetings and supervision sessions.
16. To update knowledge of the work by participating in workshops and training sessions, and sharing knowledge gained with colleagues.
17. To support and contribute to students and volunteers on placement.
18. To be aware of, and implement the Borough's policies and procedures.
19. To be familiar with the procedures for firedrill.   *continued*

20 To ensure all medications, medical care and special diets are administered.
21 To maintain appropriate health and safety standards.
22 To be responsible for the care and maintenance of the play equipment.
23 To remain with the officer-in-charge after the nursery closes, if necessary e.g. uncollected child, or a situation involving reception into care.
24 Any other duties, at a similar level, as required by the officer-in-charge.
25 The postholder must at all times carry out his/her job responsibilities with due regard to the Council's Equal Opportunities Policy.

Prepared by: . . . .   **Date:** . . . .

Agreed by Chief Officer: . . . .   **Date:** . . . .

Agreed by Postholder: . . . .   **Date:** . . . .

Stork Day Nurseries

Job description

NURSERY MANAGER

Reports to: Operations Manager and Personnel Manager

Stork Day Nurseries recognizes the trust placed in the Company by parents of the children in our care. Accordingly, we expect the highest standards of professionalism, attention to detail and responsibility from our staff at all times.

Duties and responsibilities

1 Child care

Ensure that a keyworker team system operates at all times, allocating the responsibility for each child to named members of staff.

Ensure that a high-quality EYFS curriculum is planned and delivered, promoting all areas of learning and children's development through a wide range of arts, crafts, games and activities.

Ensure that weekly planned activity records are kept up to date.

Ensure that all children's individual needs are met within the nursery.

Establish, maintain and develop an educational play environment which is attractive and inclusive.

Establish positive relationships with the children, enabling them to play and learn together co-operatively, increase their self-confidence and realize their creative potential.

Be responsible for the safety and well-being of the children and ensure that their needs for security, nourishment, stimulation and rest are properly met.

Maintain records as laid down by Local Authority guidelines and Stork policies with regard to the well-being and development of the children in your care.

2 Staff

Supervise the Deputy, senior and junior staff, students, trainees, ancillary staff and volunteers.

Ensure that appropriate staff ratios are maintained at all times in consultation with the Operations Manager.

Advertise, interview and appoint staff as required in consultation with the Personnel Manager.

Appraise staff on an annual basis and facilitate in-house training and team-building.

3 Parental involvement

Ensure that parents are kept informed of their children's well-being and progress in the nursery.

Meet their needs as working parents.

Maintain positive relationships with parents at all times.

4 General

Be responsible for all Health and Safety requirements, including regular checks, drills and training as appropriate.

Regularly liaise with Stork Head Office.

Implement Stork and Social Services policies.

Participate in team meetings, staff training and development, parent evenings and management committees.

Develop any knowledge or skills which would be of benefit to the position.

Remain loyal and confidential to both parents and Stork.

Hours of work: variable between 7.45 am and 7.00 pm
Working week: 37.5 hours (excluding breaks)

Further reading

Amos, J., *Writing a Winning CV: Essential CV Writing Skills That Will Get You the Job You Want*, 2nd Edition, How to Books Ltd, 2005

Bright, J., *Brilliant CV*, 3rd Edition, Prentice Hall, 2007

Corfield, R., *How You Can Get That Job*, 3rd Edition, Kogan Page Ltd, 2002

Eggert, M., *Perfect CV*, Random House Books, 2007

4 *INTERVIEWS*

This chapter covers:
- Preparing for an interview in the private sector
- The interview
- The contract
- Preparing for an interview in the public sector
- Before the interview
- The interview
- Decision time
- Contracts and the law
- Further reading

This stage of obtaining work is possibly the most nerve-wracking and worrying part of the process. You feel at your most exposed and vulnerable. Being well prepared will help you to become confident and more successful.

Preparing for an interview in the private sector

If you have been given an appointment for an interview as a nanny, you need to check that you are clear about the time and date of the interview, and have the correct address.

POINTS TO REMEMBER

- If you live fairly near, it is a good idea to make a trial journey, so as to find out exactly where it is, and how long it will take you to get there.
- If you have to cancel your appointment, for illness or any other reason, let the family know immediately.
- Let a friend or relative know where you are going, and at what time. You have to be careful. You may even wish for someone to accompany you to the house or place of interview, and wait outside until you are ready to leave.
- Look neat, clean and tidy. Decide what you are going to wear in advance, and choose clothes which are neither extremely smart, nor

extremely casual. You want to look relaxed and comfortable and able to cope with small children, avoiding too much make-up and jangly jewellery.

- It will help if you can take part in a mock interview. Perhaps a friend who is already a nanny might assist you in this.
- Gather together your c.v., any open references or testimonials, and certificates of training and education to take with you to show to the family.
- Try to anticipate and prepare answers to questions you may be asked.
- Prepare some questions of your own.
- Ensure that you arrive in good time, but not too early. If you need to freshen up, ask the person interviewing you where the lavatory is. Take some deep breaths, try to relax, and think positively.

The interview

In most instances, this will take place in the informal home setting, with just one person, or at most two. The children may well be around, and most parent/carers would be anxious to note the interaction between you and the child/ren, so even though you may be nervous, make sure you do not ignore any member of the family.

When talking to the parent/carer, make sure you are sitting comfortably, removing any heavy outer wear, and feeling as relaxed as possible. Listen carefully to what you are being asked, and answer appropriately, neither too briefly nor in a rambling manner. Take your time to consider each question put to you, and answer honestly and positively. If you find you are being asked questions which only require one word answers, take the initiative yourself, and extend the answers. If you think most of the questions you are being asked are either irrelevant or too personal, after a while say so clearly and calmly, being assertive but not aggressive. Try not to be put off if notes are being taken or recordings being made; this will only be to help the person remember your good clear answers, particularly if he or she has several people to interview.

Most interviews will contain some of the following questions:

- Do you have any child-care qualifications?
- What is your past child-care experience?
- Can you supply at least two references, that can be followed up?
- What interests you about this particular job?
- Are you in good health? Are you receiving any medication or therapy?
- How long do you see yourself working for this family?
- What are your views on: play and stimulation, food and mealtimes,

social and educational activities, toilet training, modes of discipline and control, rest, exercise and sleep?
- In what ways will you maintain a safe environment?
- How would you plan a daily routine for the children?
- How would you cope with difficult behaviour, for example, if one of the children said they hated you or, in a temper tantrum, bit another child?
- Are you familiar with this area and local child-care facilities?
- Do you drive?
- Do you smoke?
- Have you a past record of drink or drug abuse?
- Have you any objection to household pets?
- Would your religious, political or cultural views make it difficult for you to work in this household?
- If not living in, how would you travel here punctually every day?
- Do you have any special dietary needs?
- Are you prepared to have a police check carried out?
- Is this job likely to conflict with other responsibilities in your life?

If offered the job, disappointments often occur on both sides because certain difficult issues have not been adequately discussed, and people enter into a contract with different expectations. Therefore it would be sensible for you at interview to be clear about the following:
- How much housework will be required of you? (A trained nanny should be expected to take on only chores related to the children and the children's rooms and washing, whereas a mother's help by definition would take on a wider range of duties.)
- Who will provide which meals, and where will you eat?

- Will you have access to a car?
- What access will you have to a telephone?
- Will your friends, male and female, be allowed to visit you in the house?
- Have you discussed the family's views on television watching, fast/junk food, outings?
- Will you be expected to look after other children from time to time?
- What accommodation will you be given (if the job is residential)?
- How often will you be expected to babysit, and will you be paid extra for this?
- When will you be given a contract of employment?
- What arrangements will be made for payment of salary and deduction of income tax and National Insurance contributions?
- Will you be expected to keep a daily diary to share with the parents?
- Who else is living in the house?

You may not wish to ask all these questions, and some of the answers may well come about during your general discussion. There might be other things you wish to know, which are particularly important to you. It is worthwhile spending quite some time at the interview, as each family is unique, and you want to make quite sure that you will fit in well.

Most importantly, trust your instincts. You will know right away if you feel on the same wave-length as the family, and if you like the children. Do not feel you have to accept the first job offered to you, take your time, and remember all interviews are valuable experiences.

Activity
With a friend, role play an interview session between a parent and a prospective nanny, where one of the three children in the family has special needs. Prepare for this session and evaluate the questions and responses given.

The contract

When you have come to a decision, it is sensible to request a contract. If this is agreed in advance it will prevent many ambiguities and ensure that both parties have the same expectations of the role. Employers are obliged to give an employee a written contract of employment within 14 weeks. An example of a nanny contract is shown on pages 46–47. A contract should include:
- date of issue
- name and address of employer
- name and address of employee

- starting date and period of employment (if appropriate)
- place of work
- salary
- details of deductions for National Insurance contributions and income tax
- hours and time of work, plus any babysitting arrangements
- confidentiality clause
- sickness arrangements. If you are ill and living in, is there any cover for you? What are the arrangements for sickness pay? Who will look after you?
- holiday arrangements
- insurance
- probationary period and probation arrangements
- period of notice to terminate the employment, required by both sides
- any pension arrangements
- grievance and disciplinary procedures
- duties and responsibilities (on a separate sheet).

Both employer and employee should sign this document.

If you have gained employment in another country, a contract is even more important, but will differ in many respects to one which is suitable for working in the UK. The Federation of Recruitment and Employment Services will provide for its members a sample contract for those wishing to work abroad.

Nanny contract

This is the nanny contract as stipulated by the Federation of Recruitment and Employment Services (FRES). A separate contract exists for nannies working abroad.

Date of issue
Name & address of employer
Name & address of employee
Date of commencement of employment
Previous service (if any) counting towards continuous employment
Job title
Place of work

STATEMENT OF CONDITIONS OF EMPLOYMENT

Remuneration

The salary is ....* per week/month*, after/before deduction of tax and National Insurance, payable on .... The employer will be responsible for accounting for the employer's and employee's National Insurance contributions and Income Tax.

The employer will ensure that the employee is given a payslip on the day of payment detailing gross payment, deductions and net payment. The salary will be reviewed once/twice* per year on .... The employer will supply a P45 at the end of the contract.

Hours of work

Days/hours* to be worked, including any baby-sitting requirements (if appropriate), will be agreed by the employer and employee in advance and will be ....

The employee will be allowed .... free days per week and .... free weekends per month from Friday evening to Sunday evening. These hours of work can only be changed by mutual agreement.

In addition the employee will be allowed .... weeks' paid holiday in each year. In the first or final year of service, the employee will be entitled to holidays on a pro rate basis. Paid compensation is not normally given for holidays not actually taken. Holidays may only be carried into the next year with the express permission of the employer. The employee will be free on all Bank Holidays or will receive a day off in lieu, by agreement.

Duties (please specify)

Child/children's ages

Entitlements
The employee shall be entitled to:
a) accommodation
b) bathroom (sole use/shared)
c) meals (please specify)
d) use of car (on/off duty) (Petrol costs will be reimbursed at the rate recommended by the AA if the employee uses his/her own car)
e) other benefits.

Sickness
The employer will administer the Government SSP scheme in accordance with legislation. After three weeks of employment the employer will pay the employee full pay for a period of .... weeks, then .... pay for .... weeks. After that period SSP only will be due.

Pensions
The employer does not/does* run a pension scheme.

Confidentiality
It is a condition of employment now, and at all times in the future, that, save as may be lawfully required, the employee shall keep the affairs and concerns of the household and its transactions and business confidential.

Discipline
Reasons which might give rise to the need for disciplinary measures include the following:
a) causing a disruptive influence in the household
b) job incompetence
c) unsatisfactory standard of dress or appearance
d) conduct during or outside working hours prejudicial to the interest or reputation of the employer
e) unreliability in time keeping or attendance
f) failure to comply with instructions and procedures, for example being unable to drive due to driving ban
g) breach of confidentiality clause.

In the event of the need to take disciplinary action, the procedure will be: Firstly – oral warning; secondly – a first written warning; thirdly – a final written warning; fourthly – dismissal.
    Reasons which might give rise to summary dismissal include the following:
a) theft
b) drunkenness
c) illegal drug taking
d) child abuse.

Termination
In the first four weeks of employment, one week's notice is required on either side. After four weeks' continuous service, either the employment or the employer may terminate this contract by giving .... weeks' notice.

* Please delete as necessary

_____

(signed by the employer)

_____

(signed by the employee)

You will need to check very carefully that you have all the correct documentation, such as visas and work permits. You might also need a course of immunizations to protect against various illnesses. Going abroad means that you are far away from family, friends and known sources of help, so perhaps working abroad is not suitable for a first job.

Preparing for an interview in the public sector

You have written a brilliant application form! Congratulations! You have been asked to attend for an interview. This should not be too frightening an experience if you take time to prepare yourself.

POINTS TO REMEMBER

- Reply promptly, confirming that you will be able to attend on the given date. If you are unable to attend, telephone at once, explaining why, and stating that you are still interested in the post, but bear in mind that several people may be involved in interviewing you, and it might cause problems assembling them all again just for you. If you decide that after all you do not want this post, or if you have already secured a job, you must let the employer know at once that you will not be attending for interview.
- Make sure you know exactly where the interview is being held. Familiarize yourself with the journey there, and time how long it takes (unless, of course, you are travelling from one end of the country to the other).
- Try and find out how many people will be interviewing you, how long it is likely to last, and when you are likely to be informed of the decision.
- Read through all the information you have been given about the job, and try to anticipate some of the questions you may be asked. These questions should come out of the person specification you have been sent with the job description and application form. For example, the specification may state 'Commitment to the Borough and school's policy of Equal Opportunities'. You might be asked 'How would you extend the school's policy in relation to ensuring girls had equal access to all activities in the classroom?' Other common questions are: 'What are your strong points?' 'What are your weak points?' 'Why did you

apply for the job?' Be truthful, but positive, relating all your answers to the post. In discussing your weaknesses, stress how training has helped you overcome them.

- Read through what you have put on your application form and your c.v., and anticipate any questions that may come out of them, for example gaps in work history, or change of direction.
- Devise some questions that you might like to ask about the job.
- If you know someone who is already working in a similar job, you might ask him or her about interview experiences. Perhaps you might practise a mock interview together. If you are still at college, and have the opportunity to volunteer to be interviewed by someone on a management course, put yourself forward.
- Think about what you are going to wear. Avoid extremes in appearance. Wear neat, classic clothes that you feel comfortable in, and avoid too much make-up and jewellery.
- You may be invited to a pre-interview visit. Leap at the opportunity, as it not only shows how keen you are, it also gives you a chance to familiarize yourself with the staff, the children and the building, and

Make sure you arrive in good time

allows you to confirm that this is where you want to work. Although this is not the formal interview stage, you should approach this visit in a professional way.

Before the interview

Having reached your destination safely and in good time, looking cool and composed, announce your arrival at the reception desk or general office. You may have time to look around the building if you have not been fortunate enough to have been invited to do so previously. While you are waiting, have a look at the notice boards, be aware of the children and the noise levels, and get a feel for the atmosphere of the establishment. Find out where the lavatory is, in case you suddenly feel the need! Take a book with you, as even the best arranged schedules can go adrift, but make sure you are not hampered by unnecessary bags and clutter.

Obviously, you know not to smoke on the premises, and you should make sure that you have eaten before you leave home.

Take copies of your application form and c.v. with you, together with the job description, the person specification and any information about the establishment. You should take the originals of any certificates of qualification or education with you. Allow them to be photocopied, but make sure you take them home.

Try to relax, take some deep breaths before entering the interview room, and think positively. Remember, you have done very well to be short-listed, and all interviews are good experiences.

The interview

Enter the room in a positive and confident way, looking cheerful and relaxed. You will be asked to sit in a particular place. There will be two or more people in the room. Be prepared to shake hands firmly if one of the interviewers initiates it. There will be a short time spent on small talk, trying to put you at your ease. You should be introduced to the people on the interview panel by the person chairing the interviews and the format of the interview will be explained to you. For example, 'We will ask you questions in turn, and you will then have an opportunity to ask us questions. We hope to make a decision today so, at the end of the interview, you may either wait outside until all the candidates have been seen, or you may go home and we will telephone you later.' Initial questions may be personal to you, concerning your c.v., experience and education. Equal opportunity dictates that all candidates are asked the same questions. To put you at ease, the first question may be a very general one, asking you to give an account of your child-care experience to date, so have a well-prepared summary or your c.v. in front of you as an *aide-mémoire*. You will probably be asked what you think you can offer the establishment and your reasons for applying for the post. All the questions will relate to the person specification.

Answer all questions fully and honestly, extending your answers where you can, without falling into the trap of going off at a tangent. Take your time to consider what you are going to say, do not allow yourself to be hurried. Remember you are showing the panel how lucky they are to have the opportunity of employing someone with your skills, initiative and enthusiasm. When asked why you are applying for the job it will show you in a better light if you tell them how well suited you are, rather than just replying 'Because the money is better' or 'I live next door'. If you do not understand a question, ask the questioner to rephrase it. Having responded to a question, you may feel that your response has been inadequate. Ask them if they wish you to expand your answer.

Whatever questions you are asked, the way that you answer is nearly as important as what you say. You need to sound relaxed, confident, positive and polite. Keep your cool even if the probing becomes uncomfortable. The other candidates will experience the same questions. Do not engage

in heated arguments. If you disagree strongly with any statement, state why calmly.

Once all questions have been asked of you, it will be your turn to ask some questions. Have the ones you have prepared on a piece of paper in front of you, and ask them if the answers have not already become obvious. There may well be something else that you now wish to ask. The first question should be about the job and the establishment.

Here are some examples of questions.

- What are the roles of the other people in the team in which I will be working?
- What in-service training and staff development opportunities will be available to me?
- Is there an appraisal scheme in operation?
- What are the terms and conditions of service?

Having asked your questions, the chair of the panel will close the interview, thank you for coming and enquire whether or not you are a serious candidate for the post, and would you accept it if it is offered to you. A few candidates opt out at this stage. Remember to thank the panel for interviewing you as you leave the room.

BODY LANGUAGE

Whatever type of interview you attend, your appearance and speech will tell the panel a great deal about you. Your body language will also convey messages. What you say should fit with your body language, otherwise the employer will be very confused and perhaps not believe what you are saying.

POINTS TO REMEMBER

- When you enter the room, put your belongings away from you, stand up straight, walk slowly into the room to help you stay calm, and use a firm, not limp handshake.
- Make yourself comfortable as you sit down. Sit back in the chair, and try to relax.
- Look pleasant, but do not grin inanely.
- Do not be over-familiar with the interviewers. It is usual to address them by the names they have given you.
- Make eye contact when responding to a question.
- Do not put your hand across your mouth.

- If your hands are shaking, keep them out of sight, and do not accept a drink.
- Listen intently to any questions, showing respect to the interviewer.

Activity
Working with a close trusted friend, give a three to five minute presentation on a subject in which you are interested. Ask the friend to record your body language.

Decision time

You may be offered the job subject to references and a medical examination. Well done! Make sure you have enough information with which to form an opinion as to whether or not you wish to accept the post. You need to consider:
- whether the offer is conditional and, if so, on what
- the starting date
- the salary and subsequent increments
- the travelling time and cost
- whether there is a probationary period
- what in-service training you will be offered
- whether the conditions of service, appertaining to hours of work, holidays and sickness arrangements are fair and satisfactory
- whether the job will fit in with your family responsibilities
- whether you feel comfortable with the people and the ethos of the establishment
- whether the job will use your skills and talents enough to stretch you, and give you job satisfaction.

Contracts and the law

It is a legal requirement for an employer to state on a contract the following information:
- job title
- identity of the employer and employee
- the starting date of employment, and include any previous employment which counts towards the employee's period of continuous employment
- details of pay

- holiday entitlement, public holidays and rates of holiday pay
- details of normal hours of work, and overtime arrangements
- place or places of work.

An employer must also be able to provide the following information for you:
- details of any pension schemes
- period of notice required
- sickness arrangements, and sick pay
- an expiry date for fixed-term contracts
- details of disciplinary and grievance procedures
- the health and safety policy
- any other details that the employer wishes to make clear. This may include training expectations, equal opportunity policies, expenditure allowances and so on.

Never hand in your notice until you have received the offer of the post in writing. You will be asked to complete a form for the prospective employer to arrange a criminal background check. This is now mandatory for any person working with children under the age of 18 years. You must declare any conviction, however long ago or whatever type of sentence you received, because you are not exempt from the Rehabilitation of Offenders Act, 1974.

If you do not succeed at your first attempt at interview, try not to be too disappointed. There are several steps you can take.
- Write down the details of the interview, the questions you were asked, how you responded and if you were satisfied with your response. Recording what happened may well help you with your next interview.
- Ask for feedback, why were you not appointed? It may take courage to do this, but it might be helpful for the next occasion.
- If you feel you have been treated unfairly, take advice on taking your grievance further.
- Read about how to be an effective interviewee. Useful books are listed below.

Do not take failure too personally, there may have been much better qualified or more experienced candidates. Sometimes there is so little to choose between the best two or three applicants for a job that it is little more than luck at the end. Keep going!

Further reading

Jay, R., *Brilliant Interview*, Prentice Hall, 2007

Parkinson, M., *Interviews Made Easy*, 2nd Edition, Kogan Page Ltd, 1999

Yate, M.J., *Great Answers to Tough Interview Questions*, 7th Edition, Kogan Page Ltd, 2008

5 *MONEY MATTERS*

When you enter the world of work, there are many things to take on board about managing your money. Many of the issues discussed such as tax and insurance are complex and regulated by law. This is a brief guide to the more common issues.

Salary

It must be clearly understood, before taking up employment, what your starting salary is and the method of payment. Whether it is by cash, cheque or bank credit, your employer is required by law to give you a pay slip, notifying you of what you have earned, and detailing any deductions from your salary.

You will see from the example pay slip shown on page 56 that both gross and net income are recorded. Your gross income is your annual salary, divided either by 12 months if you are paid monthly, or by 52 weeks, if you are on a weekly wage. Your net salary is the money that you receive (take-home pay) after deductions for income tax, National Insurance (NI) contributions, superannuation and any other items you have agreed, such as subscriptions. It is your employer's responsibility to make the deductions, to add their NI contribution, and to send this regularly to the Collector of Taxes. The employers are also expected to administer arrangements for statutory sick pay and statutory maternity pay. You are expected to complete a tax return for the tax office when required, usually once a year.

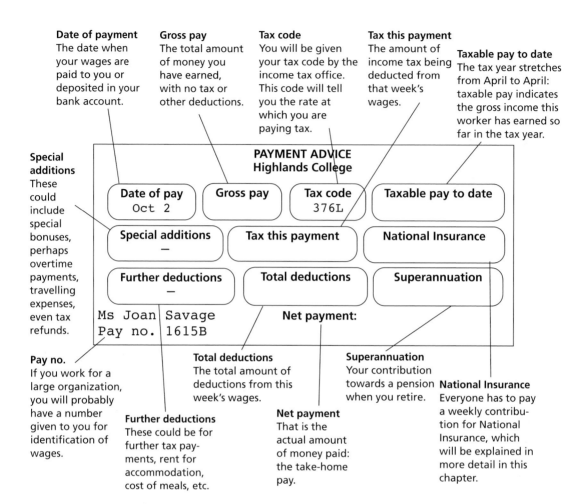

Date of payment
The date when your wages are paid to you or deposited in your bank account.

Gross pay
The total amount of money you have earned, with no tax or other deductions.

Tax code
You will be given your tax code by the income tax office. This code will tell you the rate at which you are paying tax.

Tax this payment
The amount of income tax being deducted from that week's wages.

Taxable pay to date
The tax year stretches from April to April: taxable pay indicates the gross income this worker has earned so far in the tax year.

Special additions
These could include special bonuses, perhaps overtime payments, travelling expenses, even tax refunds.

PAYMENT ADVICE
Highlands College

Date of pay
Oct 2

Gross pay

Tax code
376L

Taxable pay to date

Special additions
—

Tax this payment

National Insurance

Further deductions
—

Total deductions

Superannuation

Ms Joan Savage
Pay no. 1615B

Net payment:

Pay no.
If you work for a large organization, you will probably have a number given to you for identification of wages.

Total deductions
The total amount of deductions from this week's wages.

Further deductions
These could be for further tax payments, rent for accommodation, cost of meals, etc.

Net payment
That is the actual amount of money paid: the take-home pay.

Superannuation
Your contribution towards a pension when you retire.

National Insurance
Everyone has to pay a weekly contribution for National Insurance, which will be explained in more detail in this chapter.

Activities

To get an idea of the salaries earned by child-carers in your area, visit www.nurseryworldjobs.co.uk and use the job search facility.
What could you expect to earn:

1. As a live-in nanny with use of a car?
2. As a nursery nurse (Level 3) in a full day-care setting?
3. As an assistant in a school?

Opening a bank account

You may already have a bank or building society account and be familiar with banking systems. There are two main types of bank account: a deposit account, where money is held on which you will receive interest at regular intervals, and a current account where you can withdraw money frequently for everyday expenses. The advantages of having an account are that your employer can pay your salary with a cheque or credit to your account. Your money is safe and you can use cheques or cards instead of carrying large amounts of cash. If you are a young person, shop around, as many banks offer incentives to new customers. You will be interviewed and may have to provide references. Check out what bank charges you will be asked to pay, as these can vary considerably from bank to bank.

Income tax and National Insurance contributions

The HM Revenue & Customs states clearly that whether you work as a full- or part-time, residential or daily, permanent or temporary nanny, you are not self-employed. You are employed by the family, and they are liable to deduct income tax and NI contributions from your salary.

INCOME TAX

This is a tax payable by everyone on annual income. You can send for leaflets numbers IR33 and IR90 from the HM Revenue & Customs to help you understand how your tax code is assessed. Your employer is responsible for deducting tax from your gross salary, making returns to the HM Revenue & Customs and informing you on your pay slip the amount that has been deducted. At the end of the tax year, usually in April, your employer is required by law to issue you with a P60 statement, showing your total pay and deductions for the tax year. It is sensible to take a copy and keep both the original and the copy stored safely. If you leave, for whatever reason, your employer must give you a P45 showing your PAYE code, your total earnings so far in the tax year, and how much tax you have paid since the start of the tax year. It is very important that you have this to pass on to your new employer, as otherwise you may pay more tax than required. For a full guide to PAYE, including what to do about tax if you're starting your first job, visit www.direct.gov.uk/en/MoneyTax AndBenefits/Taxes/WorkingAndPayingTax. There are also tax offices where you can seek advice.

NATIONAL INSURANCE CONTRIBUTIONS

Your National Insurance (NI) number is your unique reference which you will keep all your life. An NI card is sent to every young person just before they reach their sixteenth birthday. It looks like a plastic credit card, and has your number printed on it. If you do not have your number, contact your local benefits agency office. Anyone over 16 working and earning at a certain level has to pay these contributions, to ensure that you are entitled to unemployment benefit, maternity allowance, incapacity benefit and, eventually, basic retirement pension. Your employer has by law to make a statutory contribution. It is the employer's responsibility to pay both contributions through the PAYE scheme. If you have any concerns over this, call the HM Revenue & Customs NI enquiry line on 0845 302 1479. You can also call the enquiry line to check the amount of NI you should be paying.

Statutory sick pay

When starting employment, it is important to check out the procedures which let your employers know when you are sick, finding out what evidence they will require, and which days your employers call your 'qualifying days'. These are usually the days in the week you work for your

employer under your contract. Always inform your employer on the first day of sickness, and keep them fully informed as to your state of recovery.

Provided your National Insurance contributions have been paid, your employer has to pay you statutory sick pay (SSP) after you have been absent from work for at least four consecutive days. This pay is subject to tax and NI contributions from you. The first three days are 'waiting days', and do not qualify for SSP. After that, the SSP payable is dependent on your gross weekly earnings during the previous eight weeks. For more information, visit: www.direct.gov.uk/en/MoneyTaxAndBenefits/Benefits TaxCreditsAndOtherSupport/Illorinjured/DG_10018786 or call the HM Revenue & Customs Employees Enquiry Line on 0845 302 1479.

Maternity rights

Under the Employment Protection Act, 1978, if you are pregnant, you are entitled to time off work for ante-natal care, can claim maternity pay from your employer, and can claim your job back after the birth. It is against the law to be sacked because you are pregnant. This would count as unfair dismissal. After your first ante-natal appointment, your employer can ask to see a medical certificate, together with appointment documentation. This right to paid time off is available to all female employees, whether full-time or part-time, whatever their length of service. For more information, go to www.direct.gov.uk/en/Parents/Moneyandworkentitlements/

WorkAndFamilies/Pregnancyandmaternityrights/index.htm. You can also call the Acas helpline for advice on 08457 47 47 47.

Superannuation/pensions

Pensions are a method of saving for retirement. By law, every working person in the UK has pension provision of some type. If you are not receiving a pension from your employer, and are not self-employed, you will receive the basic state pension on reaching retirement age. Not all companies offer a staff company pension scheme. But if there are five or more employees, your employer must offer you access to a stakeholder pension scheme. If you haven't been offered, ask your employer for details. As a nanny, you would be unlikely to be offered a pension scheme as you would only expect to work in each job for a limited period of time. However, you may consider buying into a private scheme and you could make inquiries from an insurance broker, an independent financial consultant, or a bank.

If you are working in the public sector, you will probably have some of your salary deducted as a superannuation contribution. Your employer will also be contributing. It is important when you start employment to discover details of the scheme. In some instances, it is possible to make additional voluntary contributions to boost the final pension and lump sum. If you change employment, or take a career break (perhaps to have your own children) it is not sensible to withdraw your contributions as you may well regret this at a later age, when your pension is calculated. For a full guide to pensions, visit www.direct.gov.uk/en/MoneyTaxAnd Benefits/PensionsAndRetirement. For details of superannuation, visit www.dhsspsni.gov.uk/superann-review.

Insurance

If you are working in any group setting, your employer is required to hold Employer's Liability Insurance and the certificate of insurance should be displayed in the workplace. This insurance covers the employee who may be killed or injured or who contracts an illness or disease at work. The policy carries unlimited indemnity. Employers are also required to hold Public Liability Insurance. This is the type of cover that all establishments and groups must hold to protect them against claims for damages for anyone other than an employee accidentally killed or injured (third party insurance). This provides an indemnity for sums which a group might become legally liable to pay as a result of injury to a third party and for the loss and damage of third party property. The Pre-school Learning Alliance currently recommends that settings hold a minimum level of £10m of indemnity for Employer's Liability, and £2m for Public Liability. (Some insurance companies offer a higher level of indemnity as standard.) Therefore, if you work in an establishment, you do not have to take out your own insurance to cover accidents to yourself, or accidents which may be caused by you.

If you are working in a family, your employer should also hold Employer's Liability Insurance. This is often part of your employer's household insurance policy. As a nanny, it is particularly important that you hold your own Public Liability Insurance which covers you in the event of an accident to a child in your care for which you can be held legally liable. All child-minders must also hold Public Liability Insurance, and if they employ an assistant, Employer's Liability.

An online search will reveal plenty of companies offering insurance to child carers. Organizations such as unions and the National Childminding Association often offer discounted rates to members. Some policies offer considerable extras, such as coverage for loss or damage to third party property or motor liability.

Car insurance and use of a car

You will have discussed at interview whether you are allowed or expected to use the family car. It is the responsibility of the employer to ensure that

the correct insurance cover is provided. It is sensible to get permission in writing for you to use the car. Any costs attached to your use should be met by the employer, unless there are costs due to your professional negligence, for example, if you neglect to put the child in a car seat and a subsequent injury occurs. Therefore, you need to make sure that you have your own Public Liability Insurance.

It is sensible to be clear about arrangements made for you to drive the car when you are off duty, and about payments for the petrol.

If you are contributing the use of your own car, the insurance cover must be fully comprehensive, and you must ensure that you are covered for business use: that is, transporting children. Your employer should pay you a mileage allowance along with any additional agreed sum for the extra insurance, depreciation and car tax, if it is a requirement of the employment that you use your own car.

Young children must always be secured safely in cars, whether it is your car or your employer's. It is your professional responsibility to see that car seats are age- and weight-appropriate and securely installed. If you have any anxieties about the safety of the equipment, you should refuse to drive the children until any problems have been resolved.

When using a broker to arrange any type of pension or insurance, check that they are registered with the Financial Services Authority www.fsa.gov.uk.

Budgeting

As a nanny, you may be entrusted regularly with sums of money to cover day-to-day expenses and for the purchasing of food, clothing or equipment for the children. It is important to keep accurate records of what you receive and what you spend and to meet once a week with your employer to discuss the accounts. Ask for and keep receipts whenever possible. It is better to discuss the buying of large items first with your employer, bringing home brochures and estimated amounts.

If working in an establishment which is responsible for its own funding, you may be involved in deciding which way the money is spent. Alternatively, you may be involved in collecting fees from parents, money for outings or money for meals. When handling money which is not yours, you need to be scrupulously careful. Your establishment will have procedures for dealing with money which need to be carefully adhered to. All transactions should be receipted and recorded in a book. All establishments will have an annual audit when the finances are examined. Money going astray is a very serious matter, and could lead to dismissal. If you have made an error, or are unhappy about any existing arrangements, immediately put your concerns into writing and arrange an interview with your line manager (the person in your workplace setting who is responsible for the management of you and your work).

GOOD PRACTICE

1 Before agreeing to handle money, be clear about the procedures used in your establishment.
2 Make an immediate record of any monies paid to you, and give the payer a receipt.
3 Make sure you understand the different procedures for accepting cash and receiving cheques. Immediately place the money in an agreed place of safety, before handing it over to an authorized person.
4 Ensure that you get a receipt for any money which you pay out, having first ascertained that you have the authority to commit money from the budget.
5 You need to record any payments as soon as possible.
6 Money collected should always be held and accounted for separately. Do not use it for petty cash, or for any outgoing payment.

Activity
Your community nursery has been given an unexpected donation of £5,000. How big a proportion should be spent on consumables, on visits, on furniture, on new equipment, and on books and toys? Is there anything else you would spend part of this money on? How would you manage the handling of the money and the purchasing of the equipment?

Further reading

Kitchen, G. M., *Check Your Tax*, 2008–2009 Edition, Foulsham, 2008
Levene, T., *Tax Handbook 2008/9*, Which? Books, 2008

6 SETTLING IN

> **This chapter covers:**
> - Settling in to working as a nanny
> - Settling in to working within a team
> - Employment protection
> - Further reading

Everyone is nervous and anxious before starting any new employment. You may have had the advantage of having practised settling in to your four or five placements if you have received training. You know how important first impressions are and you will arrive punctually, wearing suitable clothes, willing and eager to learn and to fit in with the family or the team.

Wherever you work, you are aware of the importance of professional behaviour and attitudes. You know that you will be reliable and punctual, contacting your employer if unavoidably delayed or sick.

All child-care practitioners, whether working with individuals or with groups of children are responsible for:

- ensuring the safety and well-being of the children
- being sensitive to the individual needs of the children
- preparing, establishing and maintaining a learning environment that encourages the all-round development of the children
- observing, assessing and monitoring the progress of all the children, and maintaining records
- regularly communicating with parents, respecting their greater knowledge of the child, and involving them in all decision making
- communicating with the line manager, whether your nursery officer-in-charge, operations or personnel manager, teacher, headteacher or employer, about the children
- participating in staff meetings and training
- ensuring equality of opportunity for all children, respecting and valuing each child as an individual.

The child-care practitioner is taking on an ever increasing role as an educator in all areas of child-care employment. You will find that you are being asked to plan areas of the curriculum for an individual child and for groups of children, to plan and evaluate activities which promote and extend areas of development, to assess progress and identify concerns, and to evaluate your own work and that of the team.

Child-care practitioners have always been seen as protectors and carers of children by the general public. Your role as an educator is still not fully appreciated. Once you are in employment, it is up to you to be more vocal about this important aspect of your work.

Values

The following statement of values by the awarding body CACHE, summarises the main obligations of those working in an Early Years setting:

The CACHE Statement of Values should underpin the content and delivery of the syllabus for these qualifications and every aspect of the assessment.

The CACHE candidate will:

- Put the child first by
    - Ensuring the child's welfare and safety
    - Showing compassion and sensitivity
    - Respecting the child as an individual
    - Upholding the child's rights and dignity
    - Enabling the child to fulfil their full learning potential
- Never use physical punishment
- Respect the parent, or those in a parenting role, as the primary carer and educator of their child
- Respect the contribution and expertise of staff in the childcare and education field and other professionals with whom they may be involved
- Respect the customs, values and spiritual beliefs of the child and their family
- Uphold CACHE's Equality and Diversity Statement
- Honour the confidentiality of information relating to the child and their family, unless its disclosure is required by law or it is in the best interest of the child

Settling in to working as a nanny

You will have met the family at interview, and perhaps since. You may have seen the accommodation prepared for you if you are residential. You will have tried to ensure that you have a contract of employment, and have clear guidelines as to the child-rearing practices of your particular family. If this is the first time you have left home, you might be missing your own family and friends, and familiar surroundings. Your employer may be aware of this, and make allowances for it. Your professionalism will not allow you to be miserable while you are working with the children, and if anyone can lift your spirits, children can.

If you are travelling to work every day, you need to ensure that you have allowed plenty of time for traffic and possible delays, for there is nothing as unsettling as arriving late on your first day.

You might find it useful, as the job is new, to sit down with your employer and complete 'The Family Routine' sheet on page 67. This will help you to understand the structure of the family's week, and your contribution to it.

The parents will find reassurance if you keep a daily diary, perhaps as outlined in the 'Daily Information for Parents' sheet on page 68. This will help you and the parents to act in partnership, meeting the needs of the children, and ensuring continuity of care.

Another useful list for you to complete is a medical and emergency information sheet like the one on page 69. You will feel happier if you have at your fingertips the names, addresses and telephone numbers of whom to contact if the parents are not available.

One of your prime responsibilities will be to ensure a safe and hazard-free environment for the children in your charge. During the first few days, in a discreet and tactful manner, you will make the following checks:

■ If there is a garden, is it safe? Check exits, contents of shed or greenhouse, storage of tools and equipment, ponds, possible poisonous plants and the unwelcome presence of animals and their droppings. Check covered sand pits, and ensure climbing equipment is secure and stable and wheeled toys are well maintained.

■ In any car used by the children, are there suitable restraints and car seats fitted?

■ At mealtimes is the high chair safe, and does it have a harness? Are there booster seats for the older children?

■ Are there stair gates, if one of the children is just learning to walk?

■ Are the pushchairs and prams in good clean condition, with harnesses attached?

■ Do the beds and bedding conform to British Safety Institute (BSI) standards?

■ What other safety equipment is available? For example, plug covers, oven guards, fire guards and cupboard catches (particularly for the cupboards where medicines and cleaning equipment are kept).

■ Check each room of the house for any obvious hazards, for example, trailing kettle leads, windows without bars or locks, frayed carpets, medicines left lying around, etc.

■ Make sure you plan routes of escape from the house in case of fire.

If there are hazards, discuss them tactfully with your employer at an appropriate time, pointing out the possible risks to the children. It may not be possible to make everything safe right away, either because of cost, or the personal views of the parents. You have done your professional duty

The family routine

	MONDAY	TUESDAY	WEDNESDAY	THURSDAY	FRIDAY	SATURDAY	SUNDAY
MORNING							
AFTERNOON							
EVENING							

Daily information for parents

	MONDAY	TUESDAY	WEDNESDAY	THURSDAY	FRIDAY	SATURDAY	SUNDAY
Sleep							
Nappy changing (bowel movements)							
Health							
Meals							
Play activities							
Social activities							
New skills							
Behaviour							
Comments and Messages							

Medical and emergency information

Mother's Name _____   Place of Work _____
Phone No.

Father's Name _____   Place of Work _____
Phone No. _____

Children's full Names _____

Dates of Birth _____

General Practitioner
Name _____   Address _____
_____   Phone No. _____

Contact if parents not available
Name _____   Address _____

Relationship _____   Phone No. _____

Hospital of Choice _____

Address _____

Phone No. _____

Children's Allergies _____

Children's Medication _____

Other relevant information

Do you know
- ❑   how to lock the house safely
- ❑   how to set the alarm
- ❑   where to find the fire extinguisher
- ❑   where to find the torch
- ❑   where to find the fusebox
- ❑   where to find the first aid equipment
- ❑   where to find a spare set of home keys
- ❑   gas, electricity, water emergency numbers
- ❑   details of car insurance.

by pointing out health and safety risks, and you are aware of what risks there are, and will attempt to minimize them, and keep the children safe. Carrying out this exercise will help you to familiarize yourself with the house and garden.

During the first week of the job, you will find yourself constantly asking your employer questions, such as 'How does the washing machine work?' 'Where does this belong?' 'Where do I find the iron?' But you will soon become familiar and comfortable with the home and the family.

Once settled you will begin to want to build a social life for yourself and the children. There are many ways of doing this. If the children are attending pre-school or school, you will meet other carers, who may be parents or nannies. If the children are friends, you may well become friends too. If the children are younger, seek out mother and toddler groups, or other facilities for the youngest children, where you will have to accompany them, thus meeting other people. Many locations where there are several nannies employed have nanny circles, where they welcome new faces. There are also some self-help groups for nannies working in more isolated settings.

It is important for you, whether you are residential or coming to work on a daily basis, to find time to discuss the day's events with the parents when they come home, but let the parents discover some things for themselves. For example, if the baby has cut his or her first tooth, it would be exciting for the parents to find out this for themselves and tell you the next day. Parents often feel they miss out on the milestones of their children's lives by going to work, and you must be careful not to make them feel excluded.

Activity
You are to work with a family of three children, aged four months, two and a half years and seven years. You will be given the use of a car. Research the various restraints that are available and suitable for the ages of the children. What other safety and insurance aspects may you need to consider?

Settling in to working within a team

An understanding of how groups work (group dynamics) will help you to settle in to your new establishment. A group is made up of people with individual personalities, different expectations and an understanding of their own role. Individuals within groups can have a major influence on the behaviour of others, both good and bad. Support and guidance and a sense of group identity may ensure the best possible child-care practice. Alternatively, negative relationships may result in poor quality of care.

If you are fortunate, you will be joining a group which has positive dynamics: a leader who with other members all contribute something to the unit and have established a way of working together co-operatively, therefore creating an ethos in which to work and provide high-quality child care and education.

Every team member will be focused on what they are trying to achieve within the establishment and what they are expected to contribute. The line management system will be clear, and each member will understand their own responsibility and accountability. In a strong team, each member will feel valued, feeling able to express problems and confident that they will be listened to. For the team to grow and develop, regular feedback is required by individual members as to their progress. The whole team will be involved in decision-making, and all the members will feel their opinions are valued.

It is always a little daunting initially settling in to such an established team, but you probably have done this several times during your training, and will have your own way of coping. As working in a multi-disciplinary team becomes more common (see page 7), it is important to ensure that you understand the roles of the other practitioners with whom you work.

GOOD PRACTICE

1 Accept your fair share of the workload, and always be willing to help when requested.

2 Use your professional skills to work co-operatively with the whole team, not allowing personality clashes or feelings of dislike to interfere with your work.

3 Ask for help and advice when necessary. Take direction, and accept constructive criticism.

4 Respect colleagues' privacy. Do not be inquisitive about other people's private lives. Always keep confidences.

5 Be aware of the working environment and respect other people's feelings with regard to temperature, light and noise.

6 Repay promptly any debts or favours given to you. For example, if someone changes a shift to suit you, be willing to do the same for them.

7 Try to support colleagues at all times, and be quick to give credit where it is due. Never criticize a team member publicly or in their absence.

8 Be ready and willing to take part in extra-curricular activities whenever possible.

9 Make a contribution to the team by keeping up to date with your reading and research. You will be respected for showing initiative.

10 Give extra support to colleagues who are under stress or unwell.

11 Always be reliable and punctual.

You will have met some members of the team at interview. You now need to get to know the other members and, of course, the children. You may be lucky enough to have a mentor allocated to you, who will be responsible for giving you information on policy and procedures, and be willing to spend time with you on a regular basis to discuss any concerns you or the team may have. The mentor will be an experienced practitioner, who is thought to display good practice. During this induction process, you should be given time to meet regularly, to discuss any concerns, to observe other experienced colleagues working and to work through an induction package.

A mentor with a new member of staff

If you have to find out everything for yourself, you might find the following checklist useful:

- the names and roles of each member of the team
- the names and dates of birth of the children
- the layout of the building and the location of essential rooms, such as the staff room, the medical room and the lavatories
- the daily, weekly, termly and yearly routines
- which children have special needs, for example those with chronic illnesses such as asthma or diabetes, or those with speech delay or learning difficulties
- the location of the first aid box, the accident book and the telephone
- fire drill procedure
- the location of the register
- the storage of equipment, inside and outside.

The more you know about the particular needs of the children in your care, the better you will be able to plan the curriculum for them. Remember that all information should be recorded accurately, and sensitive information is confidential. Records must be kept up to date and stored in a safe place. Information should not be passed to other professionals unless you are absolutely sure that they are authorized to be given access to the records. The best records are made with the co-operation of parents, who are entitled to see any reports made on their children.

Once you can find your way around, and have familiarized yourself with the day-to-day running of the establishment, you will want to find out about:

- the structure and funding arrangements
- the Equal Opportunities Policy and how it is implemented
- the Health and Safety Policy and the relevant procedures (there may be a Health and Safety representative on the staff)
- the policy identifying illnesses requiring children's exclusion
- the policy on the procedure to be followed in the event of a serious accident or illness of a child
- procedures on the reporting of suspected child abuse/neglect
- procedures for the management of children with behavioural problems
- the policy for the induction of volunteers
- procedures for bringing and collecting children
- the admissions policy and settling-in procedures
- the policy regarding the food consumed on the premises
- the policy regarding parental involvement and its implementation
- the procedure to follow if the building has to be evacuated quickly
- the appraisal procedure

- opportunities for in-service training
- times and days of regular meetings
- links with external professional workers, such as speech therapists and health visitors
- methods of assessment and recording information about the children
- arrangements for outings
- arrangements for administering medication, when necessary.

Activities
1 Imagine there is no policy to follow when taking children on out-ings in your placement. Write a policy, highlighting the proce-dures to be followed. Compare this with the actual policy in your establishment.
2 You are in charge of a sessional playgroup, and there is a waiting list for places. What admissions policies would you implement? What information would you give parents enquiring about a place for their child? How could this be presented in a brochure?

Employee protection

In addition to legislation concerning the children in your care, such as The Children Act, 1989, you should be aware of the various acts of Parliament securing your protection and rights in employment.

THE EMPLOYMENT PROTECTION ACT, 1978

This covers employment rights in relation to the following: employment contracts (employers are required to issue you with a contract within 14 weeks of starting work), minimum periods of notice, time off work, med-ical suspension, itemized pay statements, maternity rights, unfair dismissal, trade union membership, guarantee payments and redundancy payments.

Information and advice can be obtained from your local law centre, Citizens Advice Bureau, trade union or your regional branch of the Advisory, Conciliation and Arbitration Service (ACAS) www.acas.org.uk.

THE RACE RELATIONS ACT, 1976

This outlaws direct or indirect discrimination on the grounds of race, colour, nationality, ethnic or national origin or religious belief and applies to employment and training.

Advice can be obtained from the Equality and Human Rights Commission www.equalityhumanrights.com.

SEX DISCRIMINATION ACT, 1975 AND 1986

These acts make it illegal for prospective employers to take your gender into account when filling job vacancies or places on training courses. Again, contact the Equality and Human Rights Commission for more information www.equalityhumanrights.com.

Activity

Investigate and define:
- direct discrimination
- indirect discrimination
- victimization
- harassment.

EQUAL PAY ACT, 1970

This gives the right to equal pay for equal work.

HEALTH AND SAFETY ACT, 1974

This act places the responsibility for health and safety at work on employers. Advice can be obtained from Health and Safety Executive, Baynards House, 1 Chepstow Place, London W2 4TF (0171 243 6000).

ACCESS TO MEDICAL REPORTS ACT, 1988

This act gives you the right to see all medical reports made about you.

THE DISABLED PERSONS (EMPLOYMENT) ACTS, 1944 AND 1958

These acts oblige an employer with 20 or more staff to employ a quota of their workforce from a register of disabled people.

POINTS TO REMEMBER

All employees have certain basic rights:
- protection under Health and Safety Legislation
- protection from discrimination on grounds of race or gender
- protection from discrimination or dismissal for Trade Union activities
- equal pay for work of equal value

- time off on full salary for ante-natal appointments
- access to medical reports concerning employment.

When working in an establishment, you need to be clear about your role, and accept that you will be working under the direction of others, who will delegate tasks to you. You will come to understand the structure. Instructions are generally given verbally. Listen carefully, and make sure you understand what you are being asked to do. If anything is unclear or ambiguous, you must ask for clarification.

Whether you decide to work in the private or the public sector, it should not take you very long to settle in and enjoy the job.

Further reading

Cook, S., *Building a High-Performance Team*, IT Governance Publishing, 2009

Devereeux, J. and Miller, L., *Working with Children in the Early Years*, David Fulton Publishers, 2002

Kay, D. and Hinds, R., *A Practical Guide to Mentoring*, How to Books Ltd, 2007

Maginn, M., *Making Teams Work*, McGraw-Hill Professional, 2004

Nilsdotter, A., *EXCLUSIVE Nanny pay survey – The crunch is yet to come*, Nursery World, 21 January 2009

Nutbrown, C., *Working with Babies and Children: From Birth to Three*, SAGE Ltd, 2008

Sherriff, C., 'What is quality', in *Child Care Now*, Issue No. 4, 1995–1996

Slocombe, M., *Your Rights at Work Pocket Guide*, Lawpack Publishing, 2007

Stacey, M., *Teamwork and Collaboration in Early Years Settings*, Learning Matters, 2009

Vevers, S., *Major research project looks at nannies' needs*, Nursery World, 29 October 2008

7 COMMUNICATION SKILLS

> **This chapter covers:**
> - Writing skills
> - Listening skills
> - Spoken communication
> - Body language
> - Using the telephone
> - Meetings
> - Formal meetings
> - Public speaking
> - Further reading

Before starting your job you will have accumulated many communication skills. You will have written assignments and essays, recorded observations, written letters of application, listened and taken notes in class, listened and taken direction in placement, spoken in a group at college, addressed a seminar on a chosen topic, and thought about your body language and the general impression you communicate.

Writing skills

A professional person is presumed to be proficient in communicating information, ideas, directions and requests in writing and this will take many different forms. When writing for your own information, a daily diary, a list of things to remember, or a note to remind yourself to bring in certain objects for the home corner, you can record this information in whatever way is useful to you.

When writing informally to others, either within the establishment or the family, you might decide to use memoranda (memos). A memo is for internal communication within an organization. It may be a short informal note or longer with a message put across as simply and clearly as possible. It must show:
- whom it is to, and copies (c.c.) to anyone else
- whom it is from
- the date
- the subject.

```
┌─────────────────────────────────────────────────────────────────┐
│                          Memo                                    │
│  To         Linda Evans                  CC    Sue Smith         │
│                                                                  │
│  From      Jill Brown                                            │
│                                                                  │
│  Date      17.9.09                                               │
│                                                                  │
│  Subject   Outing to the park                                    │
│                                                                  │
│  I am writing to confirm that the outing to the park has been booked │
│  for 24.9.09. The nursery class will be out of the school from 10 am │
│  to 11.30 am. Three parents have agreed to accompany the staff and │
│  children.                                                       │
│                                                                  │
│                                                   JB 17.9.09     │
│                                                                  │
└─────────────────────────────────────────────────────────────────┘
```

It can be handwritten or typed. It should be initialled and dated at the end. There is a danger that some organizations may use them to the exclusion of personal direct communication. Too many memos may result in people not bothering to read them properly, or responding to directions inappropriately.

Activity
Write a memo to the school keeper or establishment manager concerning arrangements you have made for the fire service to visit the school or establishment.

It will also be necessary to write other items such as:
■ observations of the children
■ a diary to share with the family
■ reports concerning accidents or incidents
■ taking and recording telephone messages. When recording a telephone message, remember to write down:
■ whom the message is from, and his or her telephone number
■ whom the message is to
■ date and time call was received
■ the subject of the actual message
■ your name, as the receiver of the message.

Telephone Message	
To	Karen Smith
Date/Time	10.15 am 3.10.09
From	Abots Toy Shop. 0171-296-3143
Message	Equipment will be delivered tomorrow (4.10.09). Please phone to confirm.
Taken by	June Edwards

WRITING MORE FORMALLY

Any correspondence sent from the establishment must be with the approval and permission of your line manager.

You may find yourself writing:

- a facsimile (fax)
- letters to individual parents
- circular letters to all parents, such as fundraising letters
- leaflets

- reports to external organizations, such as case conferences
- assessments and recording of children's development to be passed on to the next school or the parent/carer
- letters to your line manager
- minutes of meetings
- agendas for meetings
- emails
- text messages.

Whatever you are writing, remember to:

- be clear about the purpose of your correspondence
- use short sentences, that convey your exact meaning
- check the spelling and the grammar
- keep a copy (use a black pen as this will photocopy well)
- be as neat and legible as possible (the word processor is a great help)
- date all correspondence
- be professional, sticking to the facts and being objective
- avoid jargon and terms not necessarily understood by the recipient.

SENDING EMAILS AND TEXT MESSAGES

It's becoming more common for settings to offer to email parents some written information, such as newsletters and notices. This is environmentally friendly and cost effective (as it saves paper and printing costs). Email addresses should be treated as confidential, so it's good practice to use the option which allows you to 'hide' the email addresses of the recipients of round-robin emails.

Some settings may send occasional text messages to remind parents of events. For example, 'Reminder: the nursery party is at 3–5pm this Saturday.' Large settings may also send text reminders to staff, for example, 'It's Children in Need tomorrow – don't forget your fancy dress!' Mobile phone numbers should be kept confidential.

Listening skills

When communicating it is as important to develop your listening skills as your oral skills. Being a 'good' listener does not come naturally to everyone. You need to listen carefully to others, concentrate, look interested and not interrupt, never finishing sentences for the speaker. This is especially true when listening to children, who may take longer to put over their ideas than adults. Give them time. Ask questions if you need more information.

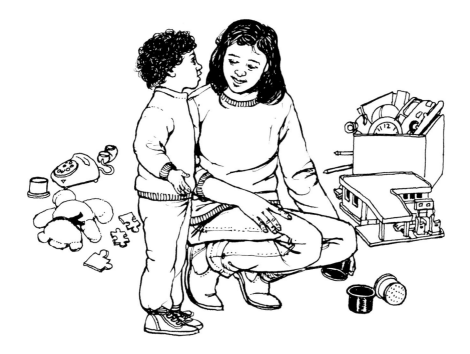

Remember that in some circumstances you may not be listening effectively. If you are worried or upset about something, your concentration may be diverted. You may be distracted by other noises or movements in the room. Your feelings about the person may distort what you hear.

Listening is a positive activity and therefore the good listener does not relax when listening, but has to monitor and analyse what is being said in order to make an appropriate response. It may be necessary to indicate to the speaker that you are listening attentively by use of words such as 'Uhuh' and 'Mmm', which display interest and understanding. Sometimes, summarizing what the speaker has just said (paraphrasing) is helpful, as it makes you listen carefully, lets the speaker know if the message was communicated correctly and eliminates misunderstanding which might lead to conflict.

Spoken communication

There is no better way of communicating than talking with people. This helps build relationships which the use of memos, faxes and email can never do. Always speak clearly, slowly and expressively, particularly when in formal situations or when the information you have to convey is particularly important. You will be using speech in informal day-to-day conversations, with your friends and colleagues and with the children. From time to time you will be using speech to give instructions to others, and at other times using it in public discussion and debate, for example at staff meetings and parent evenings. Try to present one idea at a time, and make sure that it is understood before continuing.

You may be involved in professional argument, discussing current educational policies and practice. The drawback to using speech as a method of communication is that you have to make a quick response, which may be unconsidered and regretted later. Speech is generally not as precise as written language, and it is unlikely that you will keep a copy or record. Be aware of your listener's background, knowledge and feelings, and what your ideas will mean to him or her.

Some people communicate better with speech than in writing, but it may be the other way round. You will need both skills to be an effective team member.

Body language

Remember that your body is sending out messages at the same time as you are talking and listening. To be effective, all messages should be the same but sometimes communication is spoilt when body language differs from what is being said. Think about:

- your posture
- eye contact

What message is your *body language sending out?*

- facial expression
- energy level
- position of your feet and legs when sitting
- personal space
- touching others.

For example, while engaged in conversation with a colleague, positive body language would be maintaining eye contact, smiling, leaning towards the speaker, speaking at a moderate rate, and in an assuring tone. Negative body language would be yawning, looking or turning away, going off into a daydream and missing cues.

Using the telephone

People use different voices on the telephone; and the one you use to chat to your friends may be inappropriate in the professional setting. As there is often some distortion on the line, speak very clearly, a little more slowly than usual, and do not allow your voice to drop in tone at the end of the sentence. When answering the telephone, give the name of your organization, your name and role. If the call is not for you, write down the message, and repeat it to the caller to ensure accuracy. It is advisable to note the telephone number of the caller. See that the message is passed on as quickly as possible.

If making a call, immediately identify yourself and your organization, and make sure that you are speaking to the person you wish to talk to. Be clear about the purpose of your call. Personal calls should not be made from your employer's telephone unless there is an emergency.

Remember always to be courteous – you may not be seen, but you will be heard.

Meetings

Meetings range from the very formal to the informal, and if you are working in an establishment you will be involved in both. When you start work you will be informed of meetings, either by your employer, colleagues, line manager or the notice board. You will need to find out who attends, what is usually discussed, where and when they are held, how long they last, and whether they are formal or informal. There are many different kinds of meetings such as:

- nanny with parents
- child-care practitioner with parents in an establishment
- with colleagues

- with line managers
- with senior managers
- with other professionals
- full staff meetings
- case conferences
- consultative groups
- management committees
- union and professional association meetings
- public meetings.

Meetings are one of the most important forms of communication, and are essential to the smooth running of the establishment and for forging good relationships in both the private and the public sectors.

Formal meetings

Formal meetings may vary in function and style but there are items common to all forms of committees, such as agenda, agenda papers, minutes and matters arising, and the opportunity to raise any other business at the conclusion of the meeting. Meetings can be large or small but there will usually be a chairperson and someone to take the minutes. The agenda of the meeting should be issued in advance and sets out what is going to take place. For the more formal meeting the agenda has a standard form, noting apologies for absence, minutes of the last meeting, and matters arising from them. This is then followed by the items to be discussed at the meeting and concludes with any other business and the date of the next meeting. Agenda papers are additional papers supplied with the agenda to provide background information about the items which will be discussed at the meeting. Minutes are records of the discussion and decisions made at the meeting. If the group meets regularly, minutes of the previous meeting are sent out with the agenda. Written minutes should be:

- brief, but with enough detail to enable anyone not at the meeting to understand what was discussed, what decisions were made, and what action was decided
- factual
- taken in note form, but written up in complete sentences, using the past tense
- orderly, giving a logical account, and avoiding repetition.

When attending a formal meeting, prepare yourself well by reading the agenda, and the agenda papers and minutes if they are available. Think what you can add appropriately to the meeting, and what you might wish to gain. If you wish to speak, wait until there is a pause, and always address the person who is chairing the meeting.

Public speaking

Public speaking ranges from speaking up at staff meetings, presenting information, perhaps about a course you have attended, addressing a group of parents, or attending a public meeting in your community, where you feel you wish to make a particular point. At the start of any preparation consider whom you are addressing, the purpose of your talk, what you wish to communicate, and how you are going to present it. Remember to speak clearly, audibly and slowly enough so that the audience has time to take in what you are saying. Face your audience at all times, even if you are using visual aids. Try to eliminate distracting gestures; you might try practising in a mirror or before a friend, so that you are aware of any irritating mannerisms.

POINTS TO REMEMBER

- Be yourself and find your own style.
- Be positive.
- Accept that you will be nervous beforehand and try some relaxation techniques.
- Concentrate on the task, remembering that you are trying to communicate a message.
- Monitor your vocal expression, thinking about volume, pitch and speed and take your time.
- Remember to articulate your words more clearly for a larger audience.
- Avoid too many statistics. Put them in a handout to be distributed.
- Never apologize for your presentation.
- If you forget your words, pause, take a breath, remember your objective and carry on.

Communicating your thoughts to others, whether in speech, in writing or by your body language, is an essential part of your professional role and you should strive to continually improve your performance in these areas. Practice helps, and you should take any opportunity you are offered to become more skilled.

Activity
Write a report (suggested topic: 'An evaluation of an aspect of your training course'). Make a presentation of the report to your group.

Further reading

Barker, A., *Creating Success: Improving your Communication Skills*, Kogan Page Ltd, 2006

Bradbury, A., *Successful Presentation Skills*, Kogan Page Ltd, 2006

8 *WORKING WITH OTHERS*

This chapter covers:
- Working with different styles of management
- Working with parents/carers
- Working with other professionals
- Further reading

Working with children requires many skills, including the ability to develop relationships with adults. In the workplace, you will be taking on many different roles that require good interpersonal skills and an awareness of the role and function of many other people with whom you are in daily contact.

Working with different styles of management

You need to be aware that there are various approaches to running establishments. Perhaps you should think which style suits you best, and during interviews try and obtain some idea from informal discussions what style operates in any particular establishment.

The main styles are:
- autocratic, where the leaders make the decisions
- democratic, where decision-making is shared within the team
- consultative, where the team is asked for their opinion, but the manager makes the final decision
- *laissez-faire*, where the team is allowed to make day-to-day decisions about their work, and there is no strong leadership.

Many establishments may use several of the above styles, but one will be preferred and will dominate.

Activity
Consider the four management styles and outline the advantages and disadvantages of each within a day-care setting.

Working with parents/carers

Whether you are working in the private or the public sector, you will be aware of how important it is to make strong positive relationships with parents or the primary carers of children in your care.

IN THE HOME

In your initial interview and during your settling-in period, you will have become familiar with the needs of the children now in your care, and the expectations of your employer. It is vital that you maintain an excellent relationship with the children's parents, setting aside time to communicate the daily events, any problems that may have occurred, special achievements that may have been demonstrated, and short- and long-term plans. Sharing a daily diary is an excellent way of helping the parents to keep in touch with the day-to-day events in their children's lives.

IN AN ESTABLISHMENT

All existing research shows the importance of keeping parents well informed about their children's progress, and involved in understanding the aims and ethos of the child-care establishment, working with the parents in all aspects of decision making for the benefit of the child. Involving parents in assessment and record keeping will improve the reliability and validity of the procedure. Now that you are working and in regular contact with parents, you may well be approached for support and advice. Remember the rules of confidentiality. Offer what help is appropriate. In some cases it may be more helpful to refer the parents to your line manager or other agencies.

Depending on the management style of your particular establishment, you may have a great deal of contact with parents, or practically none. On the one hand, you may be asked to visit the child in his or her home before he or she starts at the nursery, you may be inviting parents to take part in the provision of day-to-day activities, you may meet them in management meetings or parent associations, and you may involve them in

many outside activities such as taking the children swimming. On the other hand, you may find that your only contact with parents is in discussing different ways of fundraising.

GOOD PRACTICE

1 The establishment should have a relaxed and welcoming atmosphere. The staff should positively encourage parents to stay and observe the daily routine, particularly when the child first starts at the nursery or the infant school. There should be a notice board for parents, which is kept up to date. Where appropriate, a welcome poster should be displayed in many different languages. Look critically at the entrance to the room, making sure there are no barriers to adults entering.

2 Avoid being patronizing with parents. Remember they are the experts on their own individual children. Listen carefully to what they tell you about their children. At the end of the session, try to communicate to the parent the important aspects of the child's day, sharing negative and positive situations alike.

3 Respect all parents as individuals, and learn from them different ways of child-rearing. Their practice may be different from yours but is no less valid. Be open to discussion of differences.

4 Be professional at all times and never gossip about parents to other parents or within the team. Refuse to listen to other people's unsubstantiated hearsay. If you should become aware of something which might affect the welfare of a child, go directly to your line manager. Be careful not to jump to conclusions.

5 You may be working near to where you live and be familiar with some of the parents. You must be particularly scrupulous in being aware of confidentiality.

6 A parent might wish to become very friendly with you, and see you socially outside the placement. Although very flattering, it is probably better to avoid this situation developing, as this might lead to ethical dilemmas and perhaps resentment from other members of the team.

7 When working with parents from other cultures, who do not have English as a first language, try to learn a few words of their language. There should be notices and posters in their heritage language and an interpreter should be sought if necessary. Try to make links with local community groups.

8 Parents should not be asked to help in the establishment as unpaid cleaning staff. The involvement should be positive for parents, staff and children, and needs careful planning and thought to make it worthwhile. Parents need to be clear about their role and understand the curriculum and ethos of the establishment. Make sure that all par-

ents who want to be involved in day-to-day activities are given the chance to do so, but realize that this is the choice of the parent and that some may not have the time or the inclination to take part.

9 Sharing assessments and records with parents will greatly add to the reliability and validity of such records.

10 You may be involved in having to deal with an angry parent. Listen to what is being said, keep calm and do not respond angrily yourself. If you cannot sort it out, seek the help of your line manager.

Working with other professionals

During your working life, you will be in frequent contact with other people from the educational, health and caring professions. As you progress, and assume more responsibility, this contact will become more frequent. You need, from the start, to be aware of the roles and functions of other professional colleagues.

Activity
Make a list of the professional colleagues who might visit children in a social service's day-care centre. List other professional contacts you might make yourself to help children or families in the same establishment.

WORKING IN THE HOME

You may be visited by a health visitor if you are working with young babies. You may be expected by the parents to take the children to the Infant Welfare Clinic or Health Centre for developmental assessments and for immunizations. You may need to contact the family's GP. If the child needs specialist help such as speech therapy or dental treatment, you may have to accompany him or her in place of the parent. As more Children's Centres have opened, more child-care practitioners are experiencing a close working relationship with other professionals in a multi-disciplinary team. You can read more about this on page 10.

WORKING IN AN ESTABLISHMENT

Members of the medical profession will visit the establishment on a regular basis, to carry out medical examinations and hearing tests. The school nurse and the local health visitor may be in regular contact. Other professionals who may visit on occasion might be college tutors, speech therapists, social workers, educational psychologists, the police, educational welfare officers, school inspectors and governors.

Most of these people will come into the establishment but from time to time you may be expected to go out to attend multi-disciplinary meetings, such as case conferences, allocation of day nursery place meetings and community and voluntary groups involved in working with children.

Greet all visitors in a friendly way, and find out as soon as you can why they are visiting and who they wish to see. If you are alone in the room and have not met them before, ask for proof of identity unless you have been told to expect this visit.

Further reading

Adirondack, S., *Just about Managing*, 4th Edition London Voluntary Service Council, 2006

Bonel, P. and Linden, J., *Good Practice in Playwork*, 3rd Edition Nelson Thornes, 2009

Clements, P. and Spinks, T., *The Equal Opportunities Handbook*, 4th Edition, Kogan Page Ltd, 2009

Hobart, C., Frankel, J. and Walker, M., *A Practical Guide to Working with Parents*, 2nd Edition, Nelson Thornes, 2009

Jefferies, T., *Work matters: Personal development – Watch yourself*, Nursery World, 17 July 2008

Sadek, E., Sadek, J. and Walker, M., *Good Practice in Nursery Management*, 3rd Edition, Nelson Thornes. 2009

Stacey, M., *Teamwork and Collaboration in Early Years Settings*, Learning Matters, 2009

9 MANAGING STRESS

> **This chapter covers:**
> - Causes of stress
> - Signs of stress
> - Coping with stress
> - Coping strategies
> - Coping with conflict
> - Coping with sexual harassment
> - Assertiveness skills
> - Coping with violent behaviour
> - Further reading

Child-care practitioners often find themselves in stressful situations. You need to recognize, understand and respond to the causes of stress so as to avoid harming your health or your ability to work in a positive way with children and their families.

Causes of stress

Working on close terms with vulnerable people can generate a great deal of stress, particularly if you are working to an autocratic style of management, where you feel you have no say in the decisions which are made. You will have learnt from your work in college that there are life events which cause a great deal of stress. In your work situation stress might, among other factors, result from:

- meeting unreasonable deadlines
- threat of redundancy
- boredom
- unfulfilled ambition
- intensive supervision by line manager
- lack of support by line manager
- difficult relationships
- spending too much time on work activities
- staff shortages
- sickness

- intensive administration, leading to a great deal of paperwork and too many meetings
- taking on responsibilities which are not necessarily part of your job, but which you find difficult to refuse
- Ofsted inspections
- Curriculum changes.

Signs of stress

Signs of stress may include:
- variation in appetite
- insomnia
- tiredness or lethargy
- tearfulness
- tension headaches
- constipation or diarrhoea
- high blood pressure
- lack of concentration
- inability to decide priorities
- lack of interest in life

- feelings of inadequacy
- difficulty in making decisions
- feeling neglected, overworked, tense and anxious
- suppressing anger.

Someone who is stressed may find themselves often ill, and having to take time off work.

Coping with stress

Firstly, you have to admit and recognize that you are suffering from stress, and discover how you got yourself into the situation. In these times, there is much unemployment and those people who are working are expected to contribute more and more. It is often difficult to extricate yourself from a particularly stressful job because there are not many other jobs around and you have responsibilities and financial commitments. You must face up to the situation, be honest with yourself, look at alternative strategies, such as working part-time, job sharing and changing your career direction. If you cannot remove yourself from the situation, look for further help. Think about the following:

- a discussion with your line manager which may help you to change your pattern of work. It will be in both your interests to help you sort out what is causing you stress
- an appointment with your GP to discuss any symptoms you may have, and to find out what sources of help are available
- personal counselling to help you reflect on your lifestyle, and to make possible changes
- courses on assertiveness, time management and relaxation techniques.

Coping strategies

- Learn to say 'No' and how to express your feelings and opinions.
- Look for support from and offer support to colleagues.
- Try not to take work home, and relax on your days off and on holidays.
- Manage your time more effectively, deciding what you want to achieve, the priority you give to each activity, and the time and energy you are prepared to devote to each activity.
- Look after yourself by eating a healthy diet and taking regular exercise, and do not rely on nicotine, alcohol, caffeine or other drugs to keep you going.
- Relax in a hot bath or jacuzzi. Saunas and steam baths also aid relaxation.
- Apply heat to the body using a heat pad, or a hot water bottle. This may reduce muscular tension.

- Try a massage, using aromatic oils.
- Explore complimentary techniques, such as yoga and meditation to reduce the effects of stress. They may also boost your ability to avoid becoming stressed.
- Develop new interests and hobbies.
- Talk about your feelings to others, and recognize your achievements.
- Be prepared to be flexible, and do not live by rigid rules.
- Remember the good, positive things that have happened and do not focus on failures or difficulties.

Coping with conflict

Conflicts often arise at work, sometimes from outside forces and sometimes within a team. If the conflict, for example, is from an external decision, such as closing the unit because of financial pressure, the team will usually work well together to try and resolve this problem. If there is conflict with a parent, the team will generally adopt a professional united approach. But if the disagreement is within the team, the conflict might be more problematic, affecting the work of the team, the practice within the group and it will distress the children.

Some tension within a team may be beneficial. In working together to sort out disagreements, people may begin to understand themselves and others better, the decisions made are likely to be thought through more, and the process may be stimulating.

If conflict exists, ignoring it and refusing to discuss it can be harmful, and totally disrupt the smooth running of the establishment. Line managers will wish to ensure that:

- the issue is addressed promptly, giving people the opportunity to describe their views and feelings objectively, attempting to define the problem, and analysing how it developed
- old conflicts and arguments are not raised
- the team sits down together to list and evaluate possible solutions.

Reaching a solution may involve some compromise for everyone, and it is in the interest of the team and the children to draw up a plan and act on it as soon as possible. A knowledge of assertiveness skills will help you put across your view clearly and purposefully.

Coping with sexual harassment

Sexual harassment includes repeated and unwanted verbal or physical advances, sexually derogatory or discriminating remarks which cause offence, leaving the person humiliated, patronized or even threatened. It will undermine performance at work, job security and create a poor work environment.

Like any sort of bullying, it creates power in the perpetrator and fear and loss of self-esteem in the recipient. It becomes more difficult to stop if it is allowed to continue for any length of time. If you should have the misfortune to experience sexual harassment, remember:

- it is not your fault
- you are not responsible for this behaviour
- confront this behaviour assertively, making clear that you will take it further if it does not stop immediately
- be prepared to take up the issue with someone in authority
- seek support from colleagues, and be prepared to give support in return.

Assertiveness skills

Learning to be assertive allows you to be open in expressing your feelings and needs, and encourages you to stand up for your rights and the rights of others. It has nothing to do with aggression, but is a technique which allows you to relate to others in an open and honest way, discussing problems and not personalities. Your assertive behaviour should encourage others to be assertive.

Being assertive will enable you to:

- handle conflict, dealing with difficult situations, where people are angry or upset
- be more confident, decisive and comfortable in your role
- communicate better, feeling able to express your views, identify problems, and work together with other people in finding solutions
- reduce levels of stress
- develop professionally and personally.

Activities

1 Write down what you think you should expect from others in the course of a working day. Your list may include some of the following: the right to a fair hearing, to be treated with respect, to ask others for help, to say 'No', to be an individual.

2 You have been left with the task of cleaning the rabbit hutch for the past six months. You feel this is unfair. How would you express your feelings to your line manager?

3 You have recently started employment in a nursery school and are concerned that the children are not allowed to play freely inside and outside. How might you raise this issue at a team meeting?

Once you are clear about your expectations, they become easier to defend. Once you start to assert yourself, the approach is simple. You state your needs, rights and opinions in a clear way without qualification.

1 Be natural. When asking for things or giving instructions, do not apologize or justify yourself. Ask politely and keep it short and to the point.
2 Do not attempt to flatter or manipulate other people.
3 Accept it when other people say 'No', and do not take it personally.
4 If you say 'No', give a reason, but do not apologize. Be calm and warm to show you are not angry or unhappy.
5 If you are interrupted, stay calm, and continue to speak until you have finished.
6 Follow general rules of behaviour at meetings, always speaking 'through the chair'.

Coping with violent behaviour

This is a rare occurrence but if you feel threatened, you should report the fact to your line manager immediately. Do:

- remember your safety comes first
- report all incidents
- express your concerns and fears
- seek support if an incident occurs
- take someone with you if making a home visit
- refuse to accept verbal abuse.

Being aware of the value of interpersonal skills is essential in child-care employment, and will be useful to you in all areas of your life.

Further reading

Bishop, S., *Develop Your Assertiveness*, 2nd Edition, Kogan Page Ltd, 2006

Carlson, R., *Don't Sweat the Small Stuff ... and it's All Small Stuff*, Mobius, 1998

Dryden, W. and Constantinou, D., *Assertiveness Step by Step*, Sheldon Press, 2004

Palmer, S. and Cooper, C., *Creating Success: How to Deal with Stress*, Kogan Page Ltd, 2007

Wilson, P., *The Little Book of Calm at Work*, Penguin, 1999

10 PROCEDURES

During your career as a child-care practitioner, you will become familiar with regular assessment and appraisal. This is constructive and often used to establish training needs. When starting work in any establishment, you will also be made aware of other procedures, which are outlined in this chapter.

Appraisal procedures

After you have settled into your job, you will want to have some idea of how you are perceived by your employer, either the parent or your line manager. You will begin to have some sense of this by informal discussions and the comments that are made. In many establishments there will be more formal appraisal: reviewing and appraising staff performance will take place on a regular basis – generally, once a year. The purpose of appraisal is to:

- review staff performance over a period of time
- ensure staff and managers have a shared understanding of the job
- evaluate performance by looking at strengths and weaknesses
- establish future career and training development plans
- agree plans on improving any area of weakness.

The overall aim of appraisal is to establish an open and honest relationship based on trust. It should always have a positive outcome and should contain no surprises. In order to carry out a fair and balanced assessment there should be an agreed procedure. Staff should be given the date in advance, so that they have time to consider any points that they wish to raise and to look again at their last appraisal documentation. Documentation will vary from work place to work place, sometimes requiring as many as 10 different sheets of paper, and in others one simple form, as in the example on page 101. In some cases employees will be asked to complete the appraisal form themselves, and sometimes managers will complete the form prior to the interview.

Once the form is completed, you will be invited to an interview. Try to think of this procedure in a positive way, as your employer will be as anxious as you to ensure that you succeed in your job, and continue to develop new skills. Appraisal is used for focusing on your career aims and personal development. At the end of the interview a summary should be recorded. You should have the opportunity to add anything you may wish to this record. It is also helpful to write down targets which have been set and further needs, such as training, clearly identified.

> **Activity**
> Identify your short- and long-term career aims. What further training might you need to achieve your target?
> You might find it interesting to record and store this information, and refer to it again when you have been working for two years.

Grievance and complaints procedures

Grievances and complaints may occur when there has been a breakdown in communication between employer and employee, or when there have been problems in the working environment. It should be the aim of all employers to resolve any problems staff may be experiencing, as soon as possible, particularly in the interests of the children. In many establishments there is a written policy to deal with grievances. This should include:

- the opportunity to be given a fair hearing
- the right of appeal to a more senior manager against a decision made by a line manager
- the right to be accompanied by a friend or colleague when raising a grievance or appealing against the decision.

If you are working with a family, it is unlikely that there will be procedures for you to follow. If you feel aggrieved, you need to be clear yourself about the exact nature of the problem, and arrange an appointment to speak to the parent/s at a time when the children are elsewhere. Be assertive, express your concerns clearly, and you may well find that your problems will be listened to with a sympathetic ear and resolved by mutual agreement.

If you have recently left college, talking it through with your tutor might help.

Staff appraisal

INDIVIDUAL APPRAISAL AND REVIEW

Name:	Date:
Main purpose of job:	
Particular achievements in last year:	
Job skills and strengths:	
Additional skills not used in current job:	
Weaknesses:	
Job objectives found most difficult:	
Significant changes to job:	
Personal ambitions:	
New targets and objectives:	
Development needs, training, etc:	
Manager's further comments:	
Individual's further comments:	
Manager's signature:	
Individual's signature:	

Disciplinary procedures

If you are working in an establishment, you will be made aware of the disciplinary procedure, which should be available in writing. This should be fair, reasonable, consistent and easy to understand. An example is given on pages 103–105.

It is necessary to have standards of acceptable behaviour so as to ensure:

- the protection and safety of the children
- the protection and safety of the team and the parents
- the functioning of the team in carrying out philosophical aims, such as high educational standards and interpreting children's needs
- acceptable standards of practice and to prevent poor practice
- high standards of professional conduct.

It is important for all involved to understand procedures relating to conduct, such as absenteeism or harassment, as distinct from those relating to competence, such as sub-standard performance due to lack of capability.

The policy should indicate the levels of management authorized to take various forms of disciplinary action, a requirement for the employee to be informed of the case against them and an opportunity to state their case before decisions are made. There should also be a right to be accompanied by a trade union representative or a colleague at all meetings, and the right to appeal. The aim is to raise the employee's level of practice. The policy should also make clear:

- the number of warnings that should be given before dismissal
- the procedure for disciplinary hearings
- how long the warning should remain on record
- the list of offences which may result in dismissal without warning (summary dismissal is sometimes included in the contract of employment). Examples might include theft, drug abuse, fighting or smacking a child.

Dismissal

You may be dismissed if:

- you are incompetent or unqualified to do the job
- your professional conduct is unacceptable
- your job becomes redundant.

If you are dismissed and you deem it unfair or wrongful, you should seek legal advice, as wrongful dismissal allows you to bring a claim in the ordinary courts, whereas with unfair dismissal you will need to bring a claim to an industrial tribunal.

Grievance and disciplinary procedures

SUSAN HAY NURSERY WORKS LIMITED

Grievance Procedure

1. If you are unhappy about any aspect of your employment (other than the disciplinary procedure for which there is a separate system of appeal) you should raise the matter initially with your Manager. You may be required to put the details of your problem in writing.
2. Having enquired into the matter your Manager will discuss your grievance with you and will then notify you of her decision.
3. If the decision of your Manager is not acceptable, you may then refer the matter in writing to the Managing Director whose decision will be final and binding.
4. When stating your grievances you may be accompanied by a fellow employee of your choice who shall however have the right to decline to attend.

Disciplinary Procedure

1. **Purpose and Status**
1.1 The purpose of the disciplinary procedure is to ensure that the Company behaves fairly towards all its employees in investigating and dealing with alleged instances of unacceptable conduct or performance. However, this procedure is intended only as a statement of Company policy and management guidelines and it does not form part of your contract of employment or otherwise have contractual effect. Accordingly, the Company reserves the right to depart from the precise requirements of its disciplinary procedure specified below where it is expedient to do so and where the resulting treatment of the employee is no less fair. The procedure will only apply to employees who have successfully completed their probationary periods.

2. **Operation of the Procedure**
2.1 No disciplinary action will be taken against you until the matter has been fully investigated and considered by your Manager.
2.2 Disciplinary action will normally be taken by your Manager, except in the case of dismissal where only the Managing Director can take the decision to dismiss.
2.3 You will normally receive advance notice of disciplinary meetings. At each stage of the procedure you shall have an opportunity to explain the alleged misconduct or answer criticisms of poor performance.
2.4 You may be accompanied at disciplinary meetings, if you wish, by an appropriate work colleague of your choice but the colleague shall have the right to decline to attend. For the avoidance of doubt, this right of employees to be accompanied does not extend to individuals not employed by the Company and would not therefore include legal representatives or family members.

3. **Appeals**
3.1 If you wish to appeal against a disciplinary decision you should inform your Manager in writing within 3 working days of the notification of the disciplinary decision stating your reasons of appeal. All appeals will normally be dealt with speedily by the Company.

3.2 Wherever practicable, the appeal will be heard by the Managing Director and the decision shall be final within the Company.

4. **Stages of Procedure**

Minor faults will be dealt with informally but where the matter is more serious the following stages will normally be followed.

There are four stages to the procedure as detailed below being an oral warning, a first written warning, a final written warning and then dismissal. The Company reserves the right to initiate the procedure at any stage, or to jump stages, depending on the circumstances of the case.

5. **Gross Misconduct**

5.1 The following offences are examples of gross misconduct:
   - Theft or unauthorized possession of any property or facilities belonging to the Company or any employee
   - Serious damage to Company property
   - Falsification of reports, accounts, expense claims or Self-certification forms
   - Refusal to carry out duties or reasonable instructions
   - Intoxication by reason of drink or drugs
   - Having alcoholic drink or illegal drugs in your possession, custody or control on the Company's premises
   - Serious breach of Company rules as contained in the Nursery Manual
   - Violent, dangerous or intimidatory conduct

These examples are not exhaustive or exclusive and offences of a similar nature will be dealt with under this procedure.

5.2 **Procedure for Gross Misconduct**

Gross misconduct will result in immediate dismissal without notice or pay in lieu of notice. The decision to dismiss will not be taken without reference to the Managing Director. Dismissal will be notified to you in writing.

6. **Misconduct**

6.1 The following offences are examples of misconduct:
   - Bad time-keeping
   - Unauthorized absence
   - Minor damage to Company property
   - Minor breach of Company rules as contained in the Nursery Manual
   - Failure to observe Company procedures
   - Failure to report an accident
   - Abusive behaviour
   - Sexual, racial or other harassment of or unlawful discrimination against any person
   - Making unauthorized telephone calls

These offences are not exclusive or exhaustive and offences of a similar nature will be dealt with under this procedure.

7. **Incapability**

7.1 The following are examples of incapability:
   - Poor performance
   - Incompetence
   - Unsuitability
   - Lack of application
   - Unsatisfactory sickness record

These examples are not exhaustive or exclusive and instances of a similar nature will be dealt with under this procedure.

8. **Procedure for Incapability or Misconduct**

8.1 **Oral Warning**

This will be given to you by your Manager and you will be advised of the reasons for the warning and of the consequences of any repetition or failure to improve to an acceptable standard. A brief note of the oral warning will be put on your personnel record and will remain in force for 9 months. It will be disregarded for disciplinary purposes after 9 months subject to satisfactory conduct and performance.

8.2 **First Written Warning**

In the event of more serious or further misconduct or a failure to improve standards of work performance you will be given a first written warning. This will give details of the complaint, the improvements required and the time scale. It will also inform you of the consequences of failure to improve your conduct or performance to acceptable standards. A copy of this written warning will be kept on your personnel record and will remain in force for 12 months, even though any specified time for improvement has passed. It will be disregarded for disciplinary purposes after 12 months, subject to satisfactory conduct and performance.

8.3 **Final Written Warning**

In the event of more serious or further misconduct or failure to improve standards of work performance, or if the misconduct or poor performance is sufficiently serious to warrant only one written warning but insufficiently serious to justify dismissal (in effect both first and final written warning) a FINAL WRITTEN WARNING will be given to you. This will give details of the complaint, and warn that any further misconduct or continued failure to improve performance to acceptable standards will render you liable to dismissal. A copy of the final written warning will be kept on your personnel record. This final written warning shall remain in force for 18 months, even though any specified time for improvement has passed. In exceptional cases, depending on the seriousness and nature of misconduct, this period may be longer. The final written warning will be disregarded for disciplinary purposes after 18 months (or such longer period as may be stipulated) subject to satisfactory conduct and performance.

8.4 **Dismissal**

If conduct or performance remains unsatisfactory, and you still fail to reach the required standard, dismissal will normally result. You will be provided, as soon as reasonably practical, with written confirmation of the dismissal and the date on which employment terminated or will terminate.

9. **Unsatisfactory Sickness Record**

9.1 The following are examples of unsatisfactory attendance:
- long-term absence due to injury or sickness
- frequent short-term absence due to minor ailments.

9.2 In appropriate circumstances, the Company may require you to be examined by an independent medical practitioner of its choosing. In this event, you agree to co-operate with such a request and to permit the medical practitioner to discuss with the Company the findings of his examination and his prognosis for your future recovery.

The findings of the medical practitioner will be taken into account when the Company considers the kind of action, if any, which it will take against you in respect of your absence from work.

All women are protected against dismissal on grounds of pregnancy as dismissal for this reason would be found unfair, irrespective of length of service or hours of work.

It is necessary to be conversant with all these procedures, but apart from the appraisal process, the vast majority of child-care practitioners do not become involved in grievance or disciplinary procedures.

Further reading

TUC, *Your Rights at Work*, 3rd Edition, Kogan Page Ltd, 2008

1 UNIONS AND PROFESSIONAL ASSOCIATIONS

> **This chapter covers:**
> - Unions and professional associations
> - Support groups

The world of work is complex and demanding and an employee needs to develop a network of support. Child-care practitioners will find it beneficial to join a trade union or a professional association and to look in their local area for a network of people working with children.

Unions and professional associations

Every employee has the legal right to join an independent trade union. Any employer who interferes with this right can be ordered to pay compensation to the employee. Employees can belong to any trade union they like, except where membership is limited to particular occupations or skills, for instance a car mechanic would be rejected if wanting to join Voice. It is sensible to join a union or a professional association for a number of reasons. It provides a safety net in times of difficulty, arguing your case against dismissal, giving legal protection, support and advice, and will represent you in negotiating pay and conditions of service. Many unions and professional associations offer inexpensive or even free insurance cover.

A union represents its members in improving working conditions and protecting the interests of its members, for example in health and safety issues, pensions and security. It might take on a campaigning role. It will ensure that employers live up to their responsibilities to their employees.

There are three main unions generally considered by child-care practitioners.
- UNISON – the Public Service Union (www.unison.org.uk).
- Voice – the union for educational professional (www.voicetheunion.org.uk).
- NASUWT – the National Association of Schoolmasters and Union of Women Teachers (www.nasuwt.org.uk).

THE PUBLIC SERVICE UNION (UNISON)

UNISON is now the country's largest union with approximately 1.4 million members, one million of whom are women. It is committed to organize 'all those employed directly or indirectly, within those areas of employment which provide service to the public, whether in the public, private or voluntary sectors of the economy.' Among its members are many child-care practitioners, working in health, education, or the social services.

Subscriptions vary according to income and include a contribution to the political fund which campaigns for 'the retention and improvement of public services and essential industries, and other matters relevant to the well-being of members and the wider community.' You may contract out of this levy without losing any entitlement.

Some of the benefits offered by the union are free legal advice, Unison Welfare which is a registered charity to assist members in a time of crisis such as redundancy, personal injury or illness, cheaper mortgages and insurance. It publishes a booklet called *Guidelines for Nursery Nurses in Education*.

VOICE

Voice is a registered trade union. It represents the interests of professionals working in Early Years, child care and education. This includes a wide range of workers, from nursery nurses and nursery assistants to teachers, headteachers and school support staff, including assistants and administrators.

Voice differs from other unions because it positively opposes strike action and gives priority to 'professionalism'. It is not affiliated with the TUC and does not pay a levy to any political party. The many benefits include confidential legal advice and protection, personal liability insurance cover and an information service to help you stay up to date with topical issues. There are also discounts available on products such as motor, home and travel insurance. Voice also represent students on Early Years, child-care and education courses. Although not all the benefits are available to them, membership is free for students.

For professionals, membership rates vary according to employment circumstances. For full details, visit www.voicetheunion.org.uk.

THE NATIONAL ASSOCIATION OF SCHOOLMASTERS AND UNION OF WOMEN TEACHERS (NASUWT)

The NASUWT is the largest teaching union in the United Kingdom, and is open to nursery nurses who are working in education under the direction of a qualified teacher. The number of nursery nurses in this union is limited as they are only allowed to join if their contract of employment states specifically that they are required to 'teach, lecture or instruct'. It is politically independent and makes no direct or indirect donations to any political party. A range of services is offered including support, advice, legal representation, seminars and conferences. For further details and for membership fees (which vary according to your length of service and hours worked), visit www.nasuwt.org.uk/index.htm.

> **Activity**
> Define the following terms, associated with trade union action: 'closed shop', 'strike', 'victimization', 'unofficial strike', 'scab', 'lockout', 'picketing'.

Support groups

In some areas of employment there may be a sense of isolation. This can occur equally if you are working as a nanny or if you are employed in a school where you are the only nursery nurse. You may find in some urban areas that the local education authority has established in-service training (INSET) groups for nursery nurses, and thus you will have the opportunity to meet others from the same professional background to share problems and concerns, and keep up with current research and good practice. If there are no groups such as this, there is no reason why you should not contact schools in your area, offering to host similar meetings in your school, obviously with the permission of the headteacher.

Nannies working alone often feel isolated and lonely. In some urban areas where there are large numbers of nannies employed, you will find nanny 'networks' developing. This will be a social group of like-minded people who perhaps take it in turns to entertain in the family home or who organize outings, either with or without the children, in the evenings. Many close friendships are formed in this way. If you are new to an area, contacting a local nanny agency may be a way of linking into a local group.

If you are working in the country and there seem to be few nannies in employment in your village and few appropriate organizations to join, you might try putting an advertisement in *Nursery World*, inviting other nannies in similar circumstances to get in touch. Support groups themselves often advertise in the local press and in *Nursery World*.

You might consider joining evening classes to learn a new skill, a craft or a language. You could improve or update your academic qualifications. If there is no local adult education college, or it is difficult for you to be released for a particular course, you might think of enrolling for an Open University course. You would be working in isolation for most of the year, but most OU courses require you to attend a summer school, with the opportunity to meet the other students on your course.

2 MOVING ON

The most likely reason why people move on is for promotion or for a new challenge. The longer you work as a child-care practitioner, the more you will realize how important it is that you remain conversant with recent research, publications and current good practice. Your confidence and skills will be developing and you will feel the need to try a new job with more responsibility and fresh challenges.

Keeping up to date

As a professional person, you will be keeping up to date by reading current thinking and research in Early Years practice. Useful periodicals and newspapers are:
- *Nursery World*
- *The Times Educational Supplement*
- Child Education, Nursery Education and Junior Education (available by subscription from Scholastic – http://magazines.scholastic.co.uk/)
- Early Years Educator (EYE)
- Child Care magazine
- newspapers such as the *Independent*, *The Times*, the *Guardian* and the *Observer*.

Your establishment may subscribe to the National Children's Bureau, Early Years Trainers Anti-Racist Network (EYTARN) or to the National Early Years

Network. They all publish a regular newsletter and up-to-date research and information. You will continue to belong to a library, and thus gain access to new publications.

The following websites contain important information which is regularly updated:

- www.ofsted.gov.uk
- www.directgov.uk
- www.surestart.gov.uk
- www.everychildmatters.gov.uk
- www.standards.dfes.gov.uk
- www.teachernet.gov.uk

If you are working in an establishment, take the opportunity of any training offered to you. This may be during working hours or in your free time. In addition to improving your practice, you can add any courses attended to your c.v. A conscientious employer will be anxious to identify the training needs of all staff. The analysis of training needs can be undertaken at different levels:

- at organizational level, through the business plan or mission statement
- at job level, meeting the requirements of the job description
- at the employee's level, either through the appraisal scheme, or by the individual's perception of his or her personal development.

Twice a year *Nursery World* publishes a supplement called 'Training Today'. This is a good indicator of the vast number of courses on offer to child-care practitioners.

There are courses to widen your current practice, such as:

- art
- design and technology
- English, reading and writing
- mathematics and science
- music, movement and drama
- working with parents
- health and safety training
- child protection
- observation and assessment
- play
- managing behaviour
- caring for children under three.

There are many more courses available than those listed here.

If you have a child with special needs in your care, or are thinking of working with children with disabilities, there are courses run by most of the support organizations across the country. You can request details directly from them.

Record of training and attendance at courses and conferences

Date	Length of course Weeks Days Months	Funded by	Provider of training	Title	Course details	Certificate of attendance	Credit value	Comments

Record of training and attendance at courses and conferences

Date	Length of course Weeks Days Months	Funded by	Provider of training	Title	Course details	Certificate of attendance	Credit value	Comments
10.10.08	1 day	Social Services	In house	Child Protection	Recognition of emotional abuse. Procedures to follow. Coping strategies	Cert of Att.		Excellent presentation. Useful material to share with colleagues. Need a follow up on coping strategies
11.1.09	1/2 day 3 hours	Social Services	In house	Nutrition	Ethnic diets – planning menus.	Cert of Att.		Interesting, stimulating approach. More written material would have been useful.
6.6.09	1 day	Self	St John Ambulance	First Aid	Refresher to update my certificate	Yes		
9.9.09	2 yrs 6 modules	Employer. Soc Services	Holby FE College	ADCE	Registration for 5 yrs. 6 × 1 term modules Early Years Curriculum Children & families under stress Management of Early Years Provision Disability & Special Educational Needs Research Module	Diploma level 4.	1 yr off related degree.	Induction well prepared. I am looking forward to course – must think about time management and what I can research in my nursery that will benefit everyone.

To ensure that you are up to date with issues concerning equality of opportunity, the following organizations offer courses, seminars and events.

- EYTARN, PO Box 1870, London N12 0NW.
- National Early Years Network, info@neyn.org.uk
- National Children's Bureau, www.ncb.org.uk
- Positive Images, www.wgarcr.org.uk

Taking on more responsibility

This probably will not take place during your first year, but once it can be seen that you are skilled and knowledgeable you may well be asked to supervise student child-care practitioners. They may be on one of several different courses such as:

- CACHE Certificate/Diploma in Child Care and Education
- BTEC National Certificate/Diploma in Children's Care, Learning and Development
- an NVQ in Children's Care, Learning and Development
- Certificate/Diploma in Pre-school Practice
- Health and Social Care courses
- work experience for students from schools.

Having established which course your student is on, you will then need to find out the following information:

- how many students you are being asked to supervise
- the name and telephone number of the tutor
- the name/s and personal details of the student/s
- the pattern of attendance expected (days and hours)
- the expectation of the college or school, including the course curriculum and paperwork to be completed
- what links the college or school expect to make with the placement
- what training there is for you in carrying out the supervision
- what time, if any, the placement is prepared to give you to allow you to supervise properly.

It is very important that students feel welcome and comfortable, as this will help them to become confident successful child-care practitioners. You will:

- give them information about the establishment and its practices
- ensure that they only see good practice
- help them to evaluate their work and progress
- read and advise them on their written work, activities, observations and portfolios

Supervising students can be both challenging and rewarding

- advise them about resources
- meet regularly
- be honest in your assessments.

Once you have settled in a student or students, you must be meticulous in your record keeping and assessments. You will need to set aside a regular time to meet the student/s to discuss their progress and any concerns they or you may have. When carried out conscientiously, supervision work is challenging and time-consuming, but nevertheless is rewarding and can add to your job satisfaction. It is one more item to add to your c.v.

Your establishment may be involved with the delivery and assessment of NVQs in Children's Care, Learning and Development. You may be asked yourself to work towards an NVQ or you may be asked to take on an assessment role, which will entail further training.

Gaining promotion

In some settings such as being a nanny or working in a school, there will be very limited or no opportunities for gaining promotion. This work may suit you for many different reasons. If you are working in a day-care setting there will be opportunities for progressions, provided you have or are willing to gain the appropriate qualifications. Having worked for two or more years, having shown that you are a skilled practitioner and having kept up to date and attended training courses, you will be well placed to apply for a more senior position. There will be a formal process for candidates who wish to apply for the post, and the beginning of this book points out in detail how to achieve this. Being interviewed for an internal job by people who you work with and know well can be equally, or more, stressful than being interviewed by strangers.

Acquiring new skills and qualifications

Child-care practitioners working with no recognized vocational qualification can train on the job by undertaking an NVQ.

There are three levels of NVQ in Children's Care, Learning and Development – Level 2, Level 3 and Level 4. These are equivalent to other qualifications of the same level, for instance the NVQ Level 2 in Children's Care, Learning and Development is equivalent to the CACHE Level 2 in Child Care and Education. It is the Level of the qualification that dictates the position practitioners may hold. **Level 2** was designed for staff who work under the supervision of others. **Level 3** was designed for staff who work without supervision (such as practitioners who provide home-based child care) and those who supervise others. **Level 4** and above was designed for managers. For further information, visit http://www.direct.gov.uk/en/EducationAndLearning/QualificationsExplained/DG_10039029.

The Qualifications Curriculum Authority (QCA) publishes a National Qualification Framework which lists all of the qualifications accredited and accepted by Ofsted as valid for practitioners working with children. (You can view it online at www.qca.) In 2009 the government published *Next Steps for Early Learning and Childcare – Building on the 10-Year Strategy*, in which they announced that the Department for Children, Schools and Families is committed to working with the Early Years sector to 'ensure that everyone working in Early Years provision has a full and relevant qualification of at least Level three (equivalent to A-Level) and consider making this a legal requirement from 2015.' Consultation within the sector is imminent, and the qualification landscape is subject to change. You can read the full publication at www.everychildmatters.gov.uk/IG00356/. Updates will also be available at this site.

STAFF DEVELOPMENT FOR STAFF QUALIFIED TO LEVEL 3 AND ABOVE

Qualified staff can add to their academic achievements by undertaking a Level 4 NVQ or professional programmes offered in further and higher education establishments – for example, a Foundation Degree in Early Years.

Foundation degrees are at Level 5 on the QCA National Qualification Framework. They are offered by colleges and universities, but they are designed for people who are working within the field they are studying. There are no set entry requirements – your prior experience and on-the-job training will be considered alongside any formal qualifications should you apply. There are several suitable foundation degrees to choose from.

You can also gain **Early Years Professional (EYP) status** (Level 6). Those with EYP are role models for colleagues working with children aged 0–5 years. They seek to improve the quality of practice within the work-force by supporting, leading and bringing about change. To gain EYP status you must meet graduate level standards.

For further information, visit:

- www.learndirect.co.uk for advice on training courses and qualifications
- www.ucas.ac.uk UCAS (the Universities and Colleges Admissions Service) for details about higher education courses and information on how to apply
- www.learndirect.co.uk for advice on all aspects of careers and learning.

Change of direction

After several years working daily with small children, you might feel you would like a change of direction. The following are some of the options you may like to consider:

- Teaching: for information visit www.tda.gov.uk
- Nursing: for information visit www.nmu-uk.org
- Hospital play specialism: for information visit www.hpset.org.uk
- Playwork: for information visit www.skillsactive.com/playwork
- Speech therapy: for information visit www.rcslt.org
- Social care: for information visit www.socialcarecareers.co.uk
- Lecturing in a college of further education: if you have your ADCE (Advanced Diploma in Childcare and Education) already, you may be able to work for your teacher training certificate part-time, while you are working. Contact your local further education college to see if they might offer you part-time lecturing.

Whatever you decide to do, it is wise to get in touch with someone who is already doing such a job and arrange to shadow them for a day or longer if possible. This will help you to get a realistic idea of the job.

Management courses

Your ambition in life might be to start your own Early Years centre. Whether you have in mind a crèche, a nursery school or a day-care centre, you will need to get some management training. If you decide to study for the ADCE, one of the modules you take may be aimed at preparing you for management. You will need this training if you are hoping to become a deputy or head of the centre where you work or at a similar establishment. The following organizations offer training, particularly in the areas of employment law, appraisal, staff development, employees' rights, business administration, and maintaining good working relationships and practices.

- National Early Years Network, info@neyn.org.uk.
- Pre-school Learning Alliance, www.pre-school.org.uk.

An excellent book to read, giving a great deal of information, is Sadek, E. Sadek, J. and Walker, M., *Good Practice in Nursery Management*, 3rd Edition, Nelson Thornes, 2009.

Self-employment

Many child-care practitioners at some stage of their career consider setting up their own establishment. You will need to consider:

- whether there is a market and what local demand exists
- whether you can raise the capital sum needed for premises, materials, staffing costs, publicity and running expenses
- what legal requirements you must meet such as insurance, VAT, income tax, National Insurance, registration, inspection and health regulations
- the implications on you, your family and your lifestyle.

Employment difficulties

You may have carefully selected a job that you think suits you down to the ground, working with the age group and the type of establishment that you feel will best use your skills and abilities. You may have been careful at interview to obtain a contract which matches the job description and have tried to establish a good relationship with colleagues, line managers and employers. You may have been meticulously professional in your approach and conduct, working conscientiously and cheerfully. In spite of every effort on your part, you may be disappointed in your progress and job satisfaction and might be finding this first choice does not meet with your expectations. If you are working in a family, this might be because:

■ the contract is being disregarded or changed without consultation
■ the child-rearing practices of the parents are not compatible with your training
■ you are suffering from home-sickness or isolation
■ you dislike the family lifestyle, values and opinions
■ your privacy is threatened and there might be conflict over your social life
■ you are unable to build up a relationship with the children.

In an establishment you might be unhappy because:

■ you feel you are not accepted within the team
■ you find the information you were given at interview about the job was misleading
■ you have reservations about the quality of care and/or education offered
■ you have not received the training you were promised.

Whether you are working in a family or in an establishment, you might wish to change employment because:

■ there is a personality clash
■ you are subjected to harassment of some kind
■ your salary is inadequate for your needs
■ you are bored, as the job is not making optimum use of your skills
■ the journey to work is long, expensive and tiring
■ you are moving away from the area.

All these are quite valid reasons for a change of job, but do try to resolve any difficulties if it is at all possible, as your prospects for another job will be greater if you can show that you have persevered for some time. You will find that overcoming initial difficulties will stand you in good stead, and be a valuable learning experience.

Is the job making the best use of your skills?

Strategies for overcoming or preventing problems

- Use the interview to get as much information as you can. Do not be hurried. If you have any doubts, discuss them, and do not accept the post unless you feel comfortable about it.
- Be assertive and discuss any concerns with your employer as soon as you can. Once you have raised the problems with the employer, allow time for the solution to be implemented. You both may have to compromise.
- Be flexible and try and see both points of view. No job is perfect.
- Remember that you are an employee and however many qualifications and experience you may have, at the end of the day no one is indispensable.
- Do not allow your job to dominate your life. Outside interests will help you to see things in proportion.

Leaving

If you are working in a family, you may or may not wish to let your employer know that you are thinking of leaving or actively seeking other employment. When you have made your decision, you will have to give the required period of notice stated in your contract. You should do this in writing and keep a copy for yourself.

You have probably become very attached to the children and to the whole family, and you will need to prepare the children for your departure carefully and sensitively. There should be no reason why you do not keep in touch, once the children have settled happily with a new nanny.

If you are working in an establishment, your contract will show the amount of notice to be given. You may or may not have discussed your seeking other employment with your line manager and your colleagues. In completing application forms you will be asked to provide your employer's name and address for reference purposes. It is acceptable, in most cases, to request that a reference is not sought unless you have been made a conditional offer, subject to the final reference.

As in working in a family, you will need to prepare the children for the fact that you are leaving. Do not shirk doing this, as however upset they may be to hear your news, they will be much more distressed if you just disappear.

Under no circumstances write your letter of resignation before you have received a written confirmation of your new job.

---

10 The Avenue
Tetford By the Water
Lincs
L1 32

20.9.09

The Headteacher
Brigworth Primary School
Lincoln
Lincs L1 3GS

Dear Ms Holdsworth,
  Please accept this as my intention to resign my post as Nursery Nurse in your establishment. My last date of employment will be 16th October 2009, which is the Friday before half term.
  I have enjoyed my three years in your school but have been offered the opportunity of a post with more responsibility. Thank you for your help and encouragement.

Yours sincerely
Bea O'Neil

Some employers and most colleagues will want to mark your departure with some sort of social gathering and possibly a small gift. It is important to allow them to express their feelings and participate in this rite of passage.

You are fortunate in having chosen child care as your career, as there are many satisfying and fulfilling job opportunities and the possibility of continuing education and training. Good luck with your career.

Further reading

Sadek, E., Sadek, J. and Walker, M., *Good Practice in Nursery Management*, 3rd Edition, Nelson Thornes, 2009

UCAS, *Progression to Teaching and Education*, 2008

USEFUL WEBSITES

4children www.4children.org.uk
Advisory Conciliation and Arbitration Service (ACAS) www.acas.org.uk
British Association for Early Childhood Education (BAECE) www.early-education.org.uk
Children England www.ncvcco.org
City & Guilds www.cityandguilds.com
Council for Awards in Children's Care and Education (CACHE) www.cache.org.uk
Daycare Trust www.daycaretrust.org.uk
The Department for Children, Schools and Families www.dcsf.gov.uk
The Department for Work and Pensions www.dfwp.gov.uk
Edexcel www.edexcel.com
Equality and Human Rights Commission www.equalityhumanrights.com
Financial Services Authority www.fsa.gov.uk
Health and Safety Executive (HSE) www.hse.gov.uk
HM Revenue & Customs www.hmrc.gov.uk
The Hospital Play Staff Education Trust (HPSET) www.hpset.org.uk
Institute of Leadership of Management (ILM) www.i-lm.com
Maternity Action www.maternityaction.org.uk
National Association of Hospital Play Staff www.nahps.org.uk
National Association of Schoolmasters and Union of Women Teachers (NASUWT) www.nasuwt.org.uk
The National Childminding Association www.ncma.org.uk
National Children's Bureau www.ncb.org.uk
National Council of Voluntary Childcare Organisations (NCVCCO) www.ncvcco.org
National Day Nurseries Association www.ndna.org.uk
National Early Years Network info@neyn.org.uk
National Playbus Association www.playbus.org.uk
Nursery World www.nursery-world.com
Nursing and Midwifery Council www.nmu-uk.org
Playgroup Network www.playgroup-network.org.uk
Positive Images www.wgarcr.org.uk
Pre-school Learning Alliance www.pre-school.org.uk
Royal College of Speech and Language Therapists www.rcslt.org
Skillsactive www.skillsactive.com/playwork
Social Care Careers www.socialcarecareers.co.uk

Training and Development Agency for Schools www.tda.gov.uk
UNISON www.unison.org.uk
Universities and Colleges Admissions Services (UCAS) www.ucas.ac.uk
Voice www.voicetheunion.org
Working in Early Years www.childcarecareers.gov.uk